Southern Africa and the United States

Southern Africa
and the United States

—⟨☼⟩—

by WILLIAM A. HANCE, *Editor*
with LEO KUPER, VERNON McKAY,
and EDWIN S. MUNGER

Columbia University Press

NEW YORK AND LONDON 1968

WILLIAM A. HANCE, Professor of Geography and Chairman of the Department of Geography at Columbia University, is the author of *The Geography of Modern Africa* and *African Economic Development*.

LEO KUPER is Professor of Sociology at the University of California, Los Angeles, and has written *Passive Resistance in South Africa* and *An African Bourgeoisie*.

VERNON McKAY, Professor of African Studies at the School of Advanced International Studies of The Johns Hopkins University, is the author of *Africa in World Politics* and the editor of *African Diplomacy*.

EDWIN S. MUNGER is Professor of Geography at the California Institute of Technology and has written *Notes on the Formation of South African Foreign Policy* and *Afrikaner and African Nationalism*.

The authors express their appreciation to the Ford Foundation and the Rockefeller Brothers Fund for their support in the preparation and publishing of the studies included in this volume.

The sincere thanks of one or more of the authors go also to Hilda Kuper, for her comments on the draft of Leo Kuper's paper, to Eugene Harrison, Joan Breslin, Margaret Hance, and others for helpful assistance and typing, and to William Bernhardt, Editor, Columbia University Press.

Contents

‍‍‍‍‍‍⤙☼⤚

Southern Africa and the United States

Southern Africa and Its Implications for American Policy

VERNON McKAY

THE CONCENTRATION of political power in the hands of the most conservative elements in southern Africa's white population has wide-ranging repercussions on American foreign policy. The actions of the South African, Portuguese, and Rhodesian governments cause African reactions that jeopardize our interests throughout the rest of Africa. They undermine our influence in the United Nations. They lead to friction among NATO allies. Suppression of Africans is eroding away the leadership of the middle class and turning the nationalist movements in southern Africa toward Moscow and Peking. The policies of the Vorster, Salazar, and Smith regimes are thus a continuous stimulant to the Soviet Union and China to renew their efforts, and are therefore an indirect irritant to peaceful coexistence between the great powers.

The world's troubles are too complex to center on the single issue of race, but most observers would agree that everything feasible should be done to prevent the polarization of conflict in southern Africa along racial lines. Relations between blacks and whites in Africa north of the Zambezi River, aside from disturbing trends on the Zambian Copperbelt, are still relatively calm despite conflicts among Africans themselves. South of the river, however, racial hostilities have already led to violence. In this area lie eight countries which cover about two million square miles or one sixth of the continent (see table). Aside from the Mozambique lowlands and the semi-desert of the Kalahari in Botswana, it is mainly a highland area of rolling plains and hills which rise to 11,000-foot peaks in the Drakensberg of South Africa. Its climate, resources, and scenery have attracted a white population of about four million, living amidst more than thirty-two million non-whites mostly of Negroid or Bantu origin.

Southern Africa

Country	Population	Area (in square miles)	Number of whites	Ratio of whites to non-whites	1965–66 budget [a] (in million $)
South Africa	18,298,000	471,445	3,481,000	1 to 4	$1,595.0
Mozambique	6,998,000	784,032	100,000	1 to 69	147.7
Angola	5,258,000	481,351	225,000	1 to 22	175.0
Rhodesia	4,260,000	150,820	224,000	1 to 18	206.4
Lesotho	857,000	11,716	2,000	1 to 428	11.7
Botswana	576,000	222,000	4,000	1 to 143	11.8
South West Africa	574,000	317,725	73,500	1 to 7	77.5
Swaziland	289,500	6,704	10,000	1 to 28	11.9

SOURCE: U.N. Department of Social and Economic Affairs, *Population and Vital Statistics Report*, Statistical Papers, Series A, Vol. XIX, No. 2, April 1, 1967, and other sources.
[a] Based on expenditures.

Today, this southern sixth of the continent is sometimes called "white Africa" or, more frequently and somewhat less inaccurately, a "white redoubt." The concept of a "white redoubt" is based on the fact that the white rulers of the four key countries—South Africa, Rhodesia, Angola, and Mozambique—have developed sufficient military power and determination to maintain varying forms of white supremacy. The other four countries—South West Africa, Botswana, Lesotho, and Swaziland—are weak enclaves or near-enclaves that are historically linked with and economically dependent upon South Africa, the bulwark of the "white redoubt." Although the latter four dependencies contain a combined total of only about two million of the thirty-six million inhabitants of the area, two of them—Botswana and Lesotho—became independent states in 1966, and a third, Swaziland, is scheduled for independence in 1968 or 1969.

Is southern Africa one problem for the United States, or several problems? Clearly it is a diverse area with many issues that require different approaches. Policymakers believe that slow progress is possible if the area's problems are treated one by one. They fear that even these small forward steps could not be made if southern Africa really coalesces into one region of widespread racial conflict. It is useful, nonetheless, to look at the area both ways—to view it as one problem and as several problems—in order to clarify its differences and its similarities.

THREE RACIAL POLICIES

The political and social evolution of South Africa, Portuguese Africa, and Rhodesia followed different paths. In South Africa the long rivalry of Boer and Briton for supremacy obscured the fact that the real conflict was between white and black until the Afrikaners triumphed in 1948 and took South Africa out of the Commonwealth in 1961. Despite minor changes since the advent of Prime Minister B. J. Vorster in 1966, South Africa clings steadfastly to rigid enforcement of racial segregation as its basic policy. It passes the sociological tests of a caste society: one is born into a group, one can marry only within that group, one remains in that group for life, and one's group has its position above or below other groups in a hierarchical social structure. Africans are bound so tightly by a network of legal discriminations that not one of them, not even the most highly educated and most talented, can escape the system unless he succeeds in leaving the country.

In Portuguese Africa, Latin racial attitudes, more relaxed than those of the Anglo Saxon world, tolerate a limited amount of racial and social mixing under a rigid system of white political domination. A class of African and mulatto *assimilados* gradually developed, numbering in 1960 about 31,500 in Mozambique and 53,400 in Angola, who were given legal equality with whites. African nationalists rejected the *assimilado* system, however, on the grounds that it attempted to turn them into "imitation Portuguese" when they wanted to be Africans. Portugal finally abolished it in 1961 after the outbreak of a violent rebellion in Angola, and gave all Africans the status of citizens under Portuguese law. A combination of internal and external pressures since World War II also induced Portugal to launch what might be termed its "Second Five-Hundred-Year Plan" of economic development—a limited effort accompanied by a considerable expansion of white immigration from Portugal into Africa. As a result, there are about 225,000 whites in Angola today, as many as in Rhodesia, and another 100,000 in Mozambique.

In 1961 Premier Antonio de Oliveira Salazar appointed a new minister of overseas provinces, Andriano Moreira, a scholar with a knowledge of African trends who, though conservative, tried to introduce reforms. He believed in greater decentralization of authority from Lisbon to the African capitals, and he favored a greater effort to provide much-needed educational advancement and political experience for Africans. As in South Africa and Rhodesia, however, political attitudes were moving to the right, and Moreira was dismissed in December, 1962, after a tenure of less than two years. South African and Portuguese leaders used to engage occasionally in mutual denunciations of each other's apartheid and *assimilado* systems as hypocritical forms of racial domination. Today, they often emphasize the need for the whites to stand together against black nationalism.

In Rhodesia a third pattern emerged. Although a narrow segregationist in his earlier career, Cecil Rhodes modified his views to advocate "equal rights for all civilized men," a doctrine he brought from the Cape into Rhodesia though South Africa was to turn away from it. In 1923 Rhodesia's whites decided against uniting with South Africa by a vote of 8,774 to 5,989, and set out to develop Rhodesia as a self-governing colony of Britain. Its leading white politician was a segregationist, Godfrey Huggins (later Lord Malvern), who also changed his mind and began to advocate a limited multiracial partnership between senior and junior partners. "I am a human being, not a cabbage," he said, "and I reserve the right when new facts and knowledge are available, to use what wit I have to profit [from them]." When he became the first prime minister of the new Federation of Rhodesia and Nyasaland in 1953, his protegé Garfield Todd succeeded him as prime minister of Southern Rhodesia until 1958. Though Todd was cautious as prime minister, he took several progressive steps for which the white segregationists never forgave him. He raised African wages, developed secondary education for Africans, fostered a multiracial university, and advocated an extension of the African franchise on a common roll.

During the ten-year history of the short-lived Federation, the segregationists gradually won more and more white support until they were able to overthrow one government after another. First, Todd was replaced by Sir Edgar Whitehead. Though more conservative than Todd, Whitehead proved too liberal for the rightists, who succeeded in bringing in Winston Field, one of their own number, two months after Whitehead told a United Nations committee in 1962 that Rhodesia would have black majority rule within fifteen years. Field, in turn, proved to be a disappointment to the extremists and was replaced by Ian Smith, who declared to the press on December 22, 1966, that one man, one vote "will not happen in my lifetime." Meanwhile the Federation had fallen in 1963, and Sir Roy Welensky, Malvern's successor as Federal prime minister, though basically more conservative than Todd or Whitehead, was repudiated by the voters when he stood for election to a Rhodesian office. Thus, as in South Africa and Portuguese Africa, political power in Rhodesia moved to the right. The business and professional elite groups who were less fearful of the rise of an African middle class lost control of the political process to the more narrow-minded artisan, farmer, and petit-bourgeois elements, many of them recent immigrants, who feared economic competition from Africans. This trend occurred first in South Africa, then in Rhodesia, and is now evident in Portuguese Africa.

The leaders of Ian Smith's government who were voted into power by this changing electorate are politicians with a long segregationist record. Though Rhodesia's deceptive propaganda often stresses the multiracialism of the country, it is essential to note that Smith and his present ministers fought Rhodesia's limited progress

toward racial partnership all the way. It is reasonable to assume
that the Smith regime, if successful in its rebellion, will attempt to
extend the South African system of apartheid into Rhodesia. In
fact, it was reported on January 28, 1967, that Smith, in announcing
plans to set up a constitutional commission, said:

The ideal for which we are striving is a system which acknowledges our
different communities and provides safeguards which will enable these
different communities to live according to their own wishes and with
adequate protection for their rights and freedoms.

This sounds so much like South Africa's prime ministers that one
wonders if Smith, who was educated at Rhodes University in South
Africa, will not attempt to remove Africans from Parliament and
put them into some form of quasi-representative body of their
own.

Thus, despite different initial racial policies at the key points in
southern Africa these policies have drawn closer together, and it is
everywhere the "white problem"—the racial attitudes of whites—
that is the greatest obstacle to progress. South Africa and Rhodesia
both have many forward-looking whites who have struggled val-
iantly for better racial policies but they have been gradually sub-
merged. In this respect it is useful to think of the whole area as one
problem, and to recognize that forward or backward steps in any of
its countries have repercussions at every key point. For this reason
it would be impracticable for the United States to try to deal with
one country entirely in isolation from the rest.

Moreover, the ways in which South Africa and Portugal are crip-
pling the United Kingdom and United Nations efforts to impose
mandatory economic sanctions on Rhodesia are leading some observers to the view that external pressure to improve conditions in
southern Africa will be ineffective unless the world decides to deal
with the white redoubt as a single problem.

Another uniformity in southern Africa, however, is its striking
build-up of white power. South Africans now contend that they
could mobilize a more or less trained army of 250,000 whites to
defend their own terrain. An additional 95,000 Portuguese troops
are now present in neighboring territories—55,000 in Angola and

40,000 in Mozambique. The much smaller Rhodesian army and air force number only 4,500, but are supplemented by 6,000 National Police and available police reserves numbering perhaps 28,500. In all three areas, the effective combination of military and police power has crippled African political movements by either jailing their leaders or driving them into exile. Small guerrilla operations continue in parts of Mozambique and sporadic though infrequent terrorist strikes are occurring in Rhodesia and South West Africa; guerrilla activity increased in Angola in 1967, partly from Zambia. The Africans in South Africa, however, are unable to put up a real fight against the regime. Spontaneous outbreaks of violence occur, but they are quickly suppressed. Exiled South African resistance leaders claim that their followers at home are eager to rise, but these claims are impossible to substantiate.

Despite the fact that the three key countries have the common characteristic of right-wing governments that have built up formidable white power machines, they still have significant differences. South Africa has enough whites to man all the country's essential services if necessary. Rhodesia and Portuguese Africa do not. In addition, the legitimacy of the status of South Africa's whites, especially the Afrikaans-speaking majority, has been established by three centuries of history during which they helped to build an economic powerhouse that could play a great role in Africa if racial and political policies based on consent rather than force could be developed. In Rhodesia and Portuguese Africa, however, a high percentage of the whites, as already noted, are recent immigrants.

Rhodesia and Portuguese Africa differ from South Africa in still another respect. South Africa is far more self-sufficient in its economy. Rhodesia, in contrast, is heavily dependent on the outside world, while the Portuguese economy is basically weak and severely strained by six years of military effort to suppress rebellions in Africa. Moreover, Rhodesia and Portuguese Africa are confronted by the open hostility of neighboring Zambia and Tanzania, while South Africa is having some success in developing correct relations with its immediate neighbors.

REALITIES OF POWER

The world has come to recognize that the key fact about southern
Africa is the power of the whites and their will to use it to maintain
white domination. For two decades it has been repeatedly declared
that South Africa is "on the eve of a tremendous explosion." The
least one can say about this contention is that the explosion is certainly having a long eve. In fact, events are forcing observers to
give more consideration to the hypothesis of a white Rhodesian
who maintains that a political group that controls the administration, the police, the secret police, and the army does not need the
support of more than 5 percent of the people, a view tested by the
experience of Portugal and Spain as well as the communist countries. South Africa, with a white group totaling 19 percent of the
population, is well over the 5 percent bottom, while Rhodesia is on
the borderline. Accurate and up-to-date census statistics might
show, however, that Rhodesian whites total only 4 percent; in any
case, the percentage of whites will continue to decline and may already be too small to maintain tight control unless Africans remain
quiescent. There is, moreover, one difference between the African
countries and the aforementioned European countries. In the European examples, whites are suppressing whites, while in Africa
whites are suppressing blacks. In the latter instance it is generally
easier to tell who your enemy is by looking at the color of his skin.

South Africa is the bulwark of the white redoubt because of the
military power, the economic power, and the will power of its
white leaders. The wave of sabotage and terrorism that erupted
late in 1961 shocked the government into taking stringent measures
of counterinsurgency. Until that date the history of twentieth-
century protest movements in South Africa had been largely nonviolent, including Gandhi's passive resistance campaign from 1906
to 1914, the African women's anti-pass campaign of 1913–20, the
strikes and boycotts by the Industrial and Commercial Worker's
Union in the 1920's, the national anti-pass campaign of 1944–45,
the second Indian passive resistance campaign of 1946–48, the Passive Defiance Campaign of 1952, and the Pan-Africanist Congress

anti-pass demonstrations of 1960 that culminated in the killing of 69 Africans and the wounding of 186 others by police fire at Sharpeville on March 21, 1960.

The failure of these efforts, along with the banning of the African National Congress and the Pan-Africanist Congress, and other Draconian measures to suppress opposition to apartheid, finally led non-white leaders to abandon passive resistance and to adopt violence as a political tactic. On December 16, 1961, a national holiday to commemorate the victory of the white Voortrekker pioneers over the Zulu army of Dinggaan in 1838, four bombs were exploded in Johannesburg and five in Port Elizabeth in acts of sabotage. These bombings were followed by perhaps two hundred other acts of sabotage and thousands of arrests during the next sixteen months until May, 1963, when government police forces gained the upper hand. Several sporadic acts of terrorism also erupted, resulting in the killing of a number of whites.

This shock naturally aroused white fears, and the government retaliated by mobilizing a formidable machine of suppression. Its success has not only paralyzed internal opposition but has frustrated external opponents of the regime. Its actions include mass arrests, the "sabotage" acts, the "90-day" and "180-day" laws and other rigorous legislation, a large expansion of various police and defense forces, the importation of arms and the building of munitions factories, the establishment of police reserves and home guards, the development of a radio network to link the country's nearly 1,200 police stations, the formation of pistol clubs to train white women to shoot, the creation of citizens' protective associations, and the selling of cans of push-button tear gas to white civilians.

Since the power of South Africa's white regime is such an important determinant in the decision by other states of what to do not only about South Africa but also about South West Africa and Rhodesia, it will now be assessed in greater detail. There are four main units of white power in South Africa. Not only have they been greatly expanded in numbers, but their training has been strengthened and they have been reorganized to work more efficiently in collaboration with each other. They are (1) the Police

Force; (2) the Permanent Forces of the Army, the Navy, and the Air Force; [1] (3) the Citizen Force; and (4) the Commandos.

Since there are no armed guerrilla bands roaming the country, the police have remained the main instrument of counterinsurgency, calling on other forces for help as the occasion demands. Police budget estimates rose from 40,800,000 rand (one rand = $1.40) in the fiscal year 1962–63 to 56,358,000 for 1965–66. The planned strength of the police force in 1962–63 was 28,104, including 13,459 whites and 14,645 non-whites. According to the *South African Digest* of June 3, 1966, the total had risen to 32,700. The police reserves, almost wholly white, rose from 12,000 in 1963 to about 20,000 in 1965–66. According to Brigadier J. A. C. Reay, assistant commissioner in charge of the Police Reserve, it could have 50,000 men in the next few years. On May 11, 1963, it was officially announced that Coloured and Indian police reserves would also be created. The Defense Amendment Act of May, 1963, authorized magistrates to call on Citizen Force or Commando units to help the police when necessary for public safety. When white citizens began to create their own protective associations, the Minister of Justice reorganized the Police Reserve in order to incorporate these citizen groups into the police. The reorganization plan called for dividing a Police Reserve into four groups: an "A" group to be absorbed into the standing voluntary Police Reserve and receive normal reservist training; a "B" group to defend homes and other private property in their own localities; a "C" group made up of employees of mines, essential municipal services, and factories; and a "D" group of reservists in the countryside.

Although the evidence for sound generalizations is inadequate, the effectiveness of the police as a counterinsurgency force has notably improved since 1960. Courtesy campaigns initiated in that year have made white policemen less abusive in their treatment of ordinary African law violators. The extraordinary powers granted

[1] Information on the South African police and defense forces is updated from material written by the author in 1963 for a chapter on "South Africa, 1961–1964," scheduled for publication in D. M. Condit, Bert H. Cooper, *et al., The Experience of Africa and Latin America,* Vol. III of *Challenge and Response in Internal Conflict,* 3 vols., American University Center for Research in Social Systems, Washington, D.C.

to the police have greatly strengthened its ability to prevent mass political protests. The Minister of Justice can ban meetings, and the presence of police and informers at those which are held discourages attendance as well as inflammatory remarks. The confiscation of the files of protest groups has multiplied their planning problems. The latest legislation controlling the movement of Africans in urban areas further increases the ability of the police to curtail political agitation. The urban townships in which Africans live must be separated from white areas by an unoccupied buffer strip at least 500 yards wide. The electricity and water supply of the African town is controlled in the white area; during certain recent disturbances the water supply of Africans was cut off. The use of police dogs has been expanded and, in 1963, the use of aircraft by the police began with the acquisition of six helicopters and later two communications aircraft.

Testimony in sabotage trials threw additional light on the wide-ranging activities of the security branch of the police in combating subversion. Microphone eavesdropping, telephone tapping, mail opening, and infiltration of protest groups by police informers are widespread. Evidence presented in one case showed that a police agent who joined the South African Communist Party was sent by the party on a mission to Moscow. Resistance leaders are isolated from their followers by house arrest, detention, deportation, or confinement to limited areas. Police torture of recent political offenders has been alleged many times; the police have been accused of becoming agents of the Afrikaner Nationalist government rather than of the law. Whether or not these charges are valid, police methods have broken the spirit of certain resistance leaders to the extent that they have turned informers against their fellow conspirators. There is evidence, moreover, that the security branch occasionally attempts to intimidate critics of the regime by unexpected calls to search their homes or offices on the eve of overseas visits. Many observers have commented on the increased efficiency of this "Special Branch" in the past five years.

It also appears that South African unofficial counterinsurgency elements, somewhat comparable to the French Red Hand in Algeria and elsewhere, are operating. The extent to which they work with or independent of the police is unclear, but South African refugees in neighboring territories have been kidnaped, and a refugee center and an aircraft in Bechuanaland (now Botswana) were blown up.

THE DEFENSE FORCES

The alarm of the government at the wave of sabotage and its overseas repercussions is revealed even more clearly in the increased budget estimates for defense:

	(in rands)
1960–61	43,591,000
1961–62	71,550,000
1962–63	119,775,000
1963–64	157,111,000
1964–65	210,000,000
1965–66	230,000,000
1966–67	255,850,000

J. J. Fouche, minister of defense, told the House of Assembly on May 28, 1963, "Our aim is to train every young man for military service, whether flat-footed or not." Shortly afterward he declared that South Africa could have 140,000 men in uniform by the end of 1964. Although government officials have frequently said that the defense build-up is designed to protect the country from possible foreign invaders, it is clear that they also have in mind the use of defense forces against South African insurgents. In fact, parts of the defense forces were called into service after the Sharpeville shooting in March, 1960, during the Republic celebration in May, 1961, and on a number of more recent occasions. In June, 1963, the Minister of Defense stated unequivocally that the first of the three main tasks of the armed forces was "to assist the police to maintain internal order." Compulsory military training for all young white men is to be introduced in 1968.

The South African Defense Force (SADF) consists of the Permanent Force, the Citizen Force, and the Commandos and includes the trained reservists in the Reserve of Officers, the Permanent Force Reserve, the Citizen Force Reserve, and the National Reserve. Although South Africa put 344,900 men in uniform during World War II, its Permanent Force has always been small in peacetime. From a total active force of only 9,019 men in 1960–61, it rose to 21,700 in 1965–66.

The three chiefs of staff of the Army, Air Force, and Navy are also responsible for the control and training of their respective Active Citizen Force units. The South African Military College at Voortrekkerhoogte, near Pretoria, provides promotion courses for commissioned and noncommissioned officers of the Permanent Force, the Active Citizen Force, and the Rifle Commandos. Academic training is provided at the Services Academy at Saldanha Bay in Cape Province, which is affiliated with the University of Stellenbosch for its degrees. Three military gymnasiums have also been established for the Army, Air Force, and Navy, where one year's training is provided for youths between the ages of sixteen and twenty-three.

The Citizen Force, a kind of national guard, is composed of volunteers and others drawn by lot. About half of those becoming seventeen years of age are called annually to serve for four years. By 1966, 55,000 men had received training in the Citizen Force. In 1961 training in the Active Citizen Force was stepped up to nine months in the first year of service and three months in each of the last three years (before 1961 it was only three months the first year and three weeks the last three years). The Active Citizen Force is trained by personnel of the Permanent Force (Army, Air Force, and Navy).

The third branch of the South African Defense Force is the Commandos, which is composed of volunteers and those white citizens not drawn by ballot for enrollment in the Citizen Force. The Commandos have a long tradition in South Africa, dating back to 1658 when the first Burger Commando unit of seven men armed with three muskets and pitchforks was formed. Traditionally they were riflemen who elected their own officers and trained with occasional target practice and an annual review of arms. They serve without pay. During the Boer War of 1899–1902, their skill in commando and guerrilla tactics kept South Africa combatant for three years against a vastly larger British Army. By 1966 there were

210 Commando units with a total strength of 51,000 men. They now receive training in the use of rifles and infantry platoon weapons, and in minor tactics. Each Commando member is allowed a free quota of ammunition and may purchase more from government stocks at reduced prices. Because of this tradition and the popularity of rifle shooting, the standard of marksmanship, according to a government source, "is among the highest in the world." An interesting innovation in the Defense Act of 1963 was the provision for Air Commandos to assist the armed forces and police in transporting troops and equipment, in reconnaisance flights, and in providing air support for the ground Commandos.

The training of marksmen begins early. The Defense Act of 1912 provided for cadet training in musketry and drill for all school-going boys between the ages of twelve and twenty. By 1956, South Africa had 500 cadet detachments with about 85,000 officers and cadets. According to the State Information Office, "The Cadet Corps was originally established . . . for the protection of the wives and children of the menfolk who were commandeered for service against hostile Bantu Tribes." The quality of cadet marksmanship is indicated by the fact that South African cadets by 1956 had twenty-five times won the King George V Trophy established in 1925 as a competition for all countries in the Commonwealth.

A final point of note is the rapid increase in the budget provision for the manufacture of weapons and munitions:

	(in rands)
1960–61	368,000
1961–62	3,341,000
1962–63	14,289,000
1963–64	23,572,000
1965–66	51,102,000

The Minister of Defense stated on March 15, 1963, that new plans called for "the manufacture locally of ninety-two major items of ammunition." These budget increases were partly motivated by a U.N. embargo on the sale of arms to South Africa.

In contrast to this build-up of South Africa's military power, the independent states north of the Zambezi not only lack the military ability to cope with it but do not have the transport facilities to move their forces to the southern end of the continent. Moreover, the internal troubles of many African states, as well as their need for all possible aid from outside powers for economic development, restrain them from external ventures. Meanwhile, the petty squabbling of rival politicians within the nationalist movements in South Africa, Portuguese Africa, and Rhodesia is a major obstacle to their success. Suffering from the frustrations of detention or exile, the Rhodesian Africans in particular present a divided front of intense factionalism which has handicapped the efforts of the Organization of African Unity (OAU) to help them, and which has led President Kenneth Kaunda of Zambia to say that "unless they come together it's going to be very difficult to give them help in the future." [2] By 1966 some states were stopping their small contributions to the OAU for the liberation of southern Africa. And some of the weak new states in southern Africa were finding it a matter of economic necessity to negotiate correct trading and other relationships with their powerful neighbor, the Republic of South Africa.

Finally, it should be recalled that the United Nations is not a promising organ for military intervention. At the peak of its operations in the Congo the U.N. had about 19,000 men there, hardly a force to compete with the white power of southern Africa, to say nothing of the financial and ideological disruption of the U.N. resulting from the Congo operation. The USSR refused to support the position of the African states regarding South West Africa in 1967 because it does not want an effective U.N. peace-keeping body. The United Kingdom will not support an all-out sanctions effort against Rhodesia because of the risk of direct conflict with South Africa. The United States does not want to take over the responsibilities of the U.K. and the U.N. And President De Gaulle plays his own French game. The U.N. may still play a useful and limited "peace-keeping" role in certain types of situations, but it is not suitable in a divided world for a "peace-enforcing" or war-making role.

REACTIONS TO WHITE POWER

As these realities of power have become more widely understood, numerous shifts in attitudes toward the white redoubt have oc-

[2] In an interview with Christopher Parker, *The Guardian*, May 30, 1967.

curred, both inside and outside Africa. Inside South Africa, the non-whites have reacted in different ways. One group of educated middle-class Africans, though still antagonized by the indignities of apartheid, are tolerating it because the price of fighting it is too high. Some of them covertly give money to the banned African Congresses, but outwardly maintain a correct attitude toward government authority. Seeing no hope of fundamental change, they are reconciling themselves to living under white domination as comfortably as they can. A similar attitude prevails among many of the chiefs in the rural areas.

Another group, however, is made up of those who react to frustration in a quite different way. No longer allowed to release their frustration by attacking apartheid, they are turning increasingly from the bitterness of despair to extreme hostility on a racial basis —a very dangerous trend for the future. Although Africans still rarely attack whites, violence of Africans against Africans is commonplace in African townships outside Johannesburg. In one of them, Soweto, about twenty Africans are murdered every weekend —a startling symbol of the country's profound maladjustment. African industrial workers generally get along well with white employees because they show the necessary deference. But South African economist Sheila van der Horst points out that, because the African worker had no status in the South African system, he derives little emotional satisfaction from his work and hence has relatively little personal involvement with or loyalty to his firm or job. Moreover, many studies by South African psychologists have shown that, underneath any outward amicability that they may show in their relations with white workers, Africans have a hostile stereotype of whites as a united group of oppressors who treat Africans with contempt and constantly humiliate them.

Outside South Africa the exiles continue their struggle, but some of them are feeling a growing ennui resulting from the frustration of their long efforts to persuade the outside world to intervene in South Africa. The extent to which those trained in other countries for sabotage, guerrilla warfare, and related activities are returning to southern Africa is unclear but probably limited. Guerrillas are likely to lose their edge the longer they are inactive.

North of the Zambezi, in the OAU, in the U.N., and elsewhere, African diplomats and others are also revising their attitudes and tactics. Some observers contend that Africans are not as impassioned about southern Africa today as the speeches of their U.N. representatives indicate. Even if this is true, however, it is most unlikely that Africans will abandon the fight. African hostility toward racial discrimination is obviously genuine and, in any case, many politicians will keep alive the attack on apartheid as its worst symbol. Moreover, though it is imperative for certain weak states in southern Africa to make economic deals with South Africa now, this necessity causes frustrations that will produce reactions later.

The significant fact today is not the passion, or the lack of it, in the African attack on apartheid but the increasingly dispassionate way in which Africans are now expanding and refining their methods, and settling down for a longer battle. It is quite true that African orators at the U.N. continue to make occasional impassioned speeches, but the passion in the speeches is often based on a rationally calculated decision that this is the best tactic to produce the desired effect.

Since Africans have learned that they cannot produce the desired effect by using their power (because it is too limited), they exploit the technique of leverage through weakness with considerable ingenuity and skill. Despite their lack of power, they refuse to behave like pawns, which seems to irritate the disciples of *Realpolitik*. In fact it sometimes impassions the latter, causing them to indulge in loose and inaccurate generalizations about "irresponsible," "emotional," "unbalanced" African practitioners of "double standards."

The more calculated and less impassioned long-range planning of Africans was clear at the U.N. Human Rights Seminar on Apartheid held in Brasilia in August and September, 1966. First and foremost, the reaction of Africans was not to give up the fight but to brace themselves for a longer struggle. Instead of talking about change in three to five years, numerous opponents of apartheid now speak of twelve to twenty-five years.

In the corridors at Brasilia the plan to take South West Africa away from South Africa was aired with the realistic appreciation that it was easier said than done. An analogy was drawn to the

Brown case in the United States Supreme Court. Though the analogy is strained, it was used to point out that today, thirteen years after the Court decision of 1954 on desegregation, the United States still has done little to desegregate schools in the South. Nonetheless the ball has begun to roll. Similarly, Africans believe, the Assembly vote of 1966 that South Africa has forfeited its rights over South West Africa has started the ball rolling. The apartheid seminar in Brasilia also revealed a number of other interesting indications of the kind of fight Africans plan to carry on in the future. One resolution asked the U.N. Secretariat to establish an anti-apartheid propaganda unit; it began to operate several months later. The groundwork was also laid for two more international conferences on southern Africa. One, a proposed governmental conference, grew out of a discussion precipitated by one of the South African exiles who emphasized the need for a coordinating body for better planning of the struggle in southern Africa, and who suggested that it should concentrate first on Rhodesia, then on Portuguese Africa, and work its way down to its toughest problem—South Africa. This conference of governments was to try to deal with southern Africa as a whole and to show the relationship between the Rhodesian, Portuguese African, and South African problems. The other is to be a conference on apartheid by labor, church, Negro, student, and other nongovernmental delegates from the countries of South Africa's major trading partners.

Another striking development in Brasilia was the time and emphasis devoted to techniques and methods of propaganda. Ronald Segal, a white South African exile who was one of the seven "experts on apartheid" invited by the U.N., told the assembled delegates of twenty-nine states that the ultimate value of the meeting would be its propaganda value. Attention was called to the prodigious propaganda efforts of the South African government and its friends overseas, and the need for effective counterpropaganda. Successful attempts were made to make anti-apartheid propaganda more effective by deleting from the Brasilia draft report a number of obvious exaggerations that would have weakened its effect by increasing its vulnerability to criticism. At the suggestion of Colin Legum, a reference to "massacres and concentration camps" in

South Africa was deleted; Ambassador Achkar Marof of Guinea obtained the deletion of a statement that "there were also manifestations of apartheid" in Angola and Mozambique; and a Malaysian representative was successful in getting deleted a statement that "South Africa had aided Portugal with arms and men in suppressing revolts in Angola."

RISE OF CONSERVATISM

The growing recognition of the imbalance between the power of the white governing groups and the weakness of the black Africans in and near the "white redoubt" has had a notable effect on thinking about southern Africa especially in England and the United States. It has encouraged a new optimism among militant conservatives who would reinforce the status quo and has deeply discouraged liberal leaders of the fight against colonialism and apartheid.

Until the 1960s, liberals had an open field in the United States for anti-apartheid propaganda. Within the past two years, however, there has been an intensive mobilization of conservative propaganda to support the Vorster, Salazar, and Smith regimes. In September, 1965, the American-African Affairs Association was formed in New York by the same group that backed Moise Tshombe and his Katanga secession movement in 1961–62, when their organization was called the American Committee for Aid to Katanga Freedom Fighters. About 15 of the 50 or more members of the American-African Affairs Association are writers or editors for the conservative *National Review*, and many of them are also involved in other conservative movements as well. Some of their publications are basically factual while others present gross distortions, such as the view that Rhodesian Africans are "a simple childlike people still blinking from the darkness of the cave" (from the April, 1967, report of a three-man "Special Fact Finding Mission" to Rhodesia).

In general, however, the American-African Affairs Association is less extreme than the American-Southern Africa Council established in 1966, which works closely with the Friends of Rhodesian Independence. Located in Washington, D.C., it is supported by the right-wing Liberty Lobby and by John Birch Society members and sympathizers. Academic Africanists are conspicuous by their absence from both these groups, although a few professors who are popular in conservative circles have joined the American-African Affairs Association.

The work of these two pressure groups devoted exclusively to Africa is supplemented by a rising exploitation of African issues, especially white redoubt issues, in a wide range of more general conservative societies and in the conservative press and radio. Supporters for these organizations come from varied and overlapping elements of American life—notably the *hard-line anti-Communist type* (including a number of former Communists, former FBI agents, refugees from Eastern Europe, and several fundamentalist evangelical ministers); the *anti-U.N. superpatriots* who regard New York and the "Eastern Establishment" as the center of an "invisible world government" conspiracy; and *anti-Negro racists* in both the deep South and some northern urban centers. In addition, support for the status quo in southern Africa has come from certain academics and prestigious Americans who regard themselves as "realists" in foreign policy matters, and who do not have any affiliation with the above anti-Communist, anti-U.N., and anti-Negro extremists.

Conservative elements in the major national churches are also speaking out on southern African issues. While it is true that the national executives of the National Council of the Churches of Christ and of the Catholic Association of International Peace, as well as of individual denominations, have adopted resolutions condemning apartheid, the new development of the mid-1960s has been the organization of small conservative groups within the major churches to adopt resolutions attacking the positions on Africa taken by these national executives.

How strong is this conservative trend? Officials in the African Bureau of the State Department generally take the position that the present situation represents a natural swing of the pendulum and that the liberal spirit of the United States is too vigorous to succumb to conservatism. They hope that the thousands of returned Peace Corps volunteers and others who have served in Africa will effectively counter the distortions of fact being spread by the extremists. They note that the pro-Smith rallies held in Chicago, New York, and Washington in the spring of 1967 were poorly attended both in numbers and in caliber of participants. At the Washington "Peace with Rhodesia" banquet on May 17, 1967, for example, the leading luminary was Senator Strom Thurmond, Republican of South Carolina, who brushed over the fact that Rhodesia's 4,500-man army and air force has trouble enough at home and declared that "Rhodesia is willing to make available, immediately, up to 5,000 troops" to aid the United States in Vietnam.

There can be no doubt, however, that conservative organizations today have far more money, more publications, larger circulation for their publications, and more radio programs than liberal groups.

These facts have been well documented by a Washington organization, Group Research, Inc., which estimates that the number of periodicals "with circulation in excess of 15,000 is almost twice as large for the right-of-center group as for the left-of-center group." The growth rate of conservative periodicals in the period from 1961 to 1965 was especially high, having received a big boost in the Goldwater presidential campaign in 1964.

Conservative radio programs are also a striking phenomenon of this decade, and they have virtually no liberal counterpart. Right-wing radio talks are heard each week on more than 10,000 broadcasts averaging more than fifteen minutes each, not including the major network programs of Paul Harvey and Fulton Lewis III. In the area of foreign policy, these conservative organizations, publications, and radio programs concentrated on Eastern Europe and Communist China in the 1940s and 1950s, and picked up the cause of the whites in southern Africa in the 1960s. One of Rhodesian Prime Minister Ian Smith's new radio friends in the United States, the articulate right-wing preacher Dr. Carl McIntyre, is heard half an hour a day for six days a week on the "Twentieth Century Reformation Hour" over more than 600 stations.

By June, 1967, the American "Friends of Rhodesia" had grown to 122 branches with 25,000 members, according to John Acord of the American-Southern Africa Council, which distributes a *Newsletter* with a circulation of 14,220 and does other public relations work for the Friends of Rhodesia. The mushrooming of these societies to support Rhodesia's little band of 224,000 whites (perhaps 70,000 families) is a phenomenal contrast to the limited organizational support mobilized in this country for the 3,400,000 whites of South Africa. How can it be explained?

One reason, of course, is that South Africa's policy of apartheid is clear cut and has become a universal symbol of injustice. Rhodesians, on the other hand, claim that they support multiracial partnership rather than segregation, though in fact the present leaders have long fought advances toward a meaningful racial partnership.

South Africans also lack another asset available to the Rhodesians. This is the intense anti-British tradition in certain American circles, including some of the Irish communities and parts of the Midwest. This audience is highly receptive to the theme that we should not support British economic sanctions against Rhodesia because the perfidious British will not support U.S. economic sanctions against Cuba and China.

The anti-U.N. group, on the other hand, is especially aroused over the Rhodesian case because the Security Council adopted *mandatory* economic sanctions toward the Smith regime, while U.N. sanctions resolutions against South Africa (aside from the 1963 arms embargo) were only recommendations by the General Assembly. This is a clear case, in the view of the radical right, of the "invisible world government conspiracy's" illegal intervention in the domestic affairs of a "sovereign independent state." This conspiracy theory is rejected by moderate conservatives, but they insist that the U.N.'s action is illegal because a threat to the peace does not exist—a plausible view.

Another asset of the Rhodesian lobby [3] is the Smith government's November, 1965, Declaration of Independence, which is modeled in part on the American Declaration of Independence and lends itself to skillful exploitation among patriotic societies in the United States. Apparently the image of a small band of sturdy and indus-

[3] Information on the Rhodesian lobby was published in modified form in "The Domino Theory of the Rhodesia Lobby," *Africa Report*, June, 1967.

trious white colonists proclaiming their freedom in language similar to that used in this country in 1776 evokes a warm response among some Americans who lack accurate information. The fact is, as affirmed in an address by Assistant Secretary of State for African Affairs Joseph Palmer on February 28, 1967:

Seldom in history have two such superficially similar acts been so vastly different in purpose and meaning. The Rhodesian document makes glancing references to "civilization" and the "principles of Western democracy," but its aims are narrow and its direction is a retreat from the main currents of the times and from the international community of nations. No broad vision emerges to inspire mankind; rather an obstinate defense of narrow privilege, based on racial bias and minority rule. The Rhodesian document is inward-looking and static, holding no promise either for progress for the majority or for creativity for the minority.

White Rhodesians also have the support, of course, of the same anti-Negro groups that back the South African government, as well as those obsessively concerned with anti-Communism. Much is written about saving "white civilization" from "black savagery" and "cannibalism," and the conservative press and radio often praise "that great anti-Communist, Ian Smith."

Finally, the organizational job of mobilizing support on the Rhodesian question has received valuable assistance from the Rhodesian Information Office in Washington. Smith's representatives, of course, had to register with the Department of Justice under the terms of the Foreign Agents Registration Act of 1938, as amended, and the political propaganda they disseminate through United States mails must be properly identified and a copy filed with the Department of Justice. Between February 1, 1966, and January 31, 1967, they received $65,053 from the Smith government for salaries and operating expenses in addition to a grant of $14,000 for publications. By April, 1967, their main bimonthly publication, *Rhodesian Commentary*, had a circulation of 12,975 copies. They also disseminate *Rhodesian Viewpoint*, a fairly frequent two-page sheet of general information with a small circulation, an interesting *Press Comment on Rhodesia* reprinting pro-Smith views mainly from the U.S. press, and numerous pamphlets and a small number of films.

Finally, they have approached many members of Congress, more than twenty of whom have joined the attack on our government's Rhodesian policy.

A major theme of the radical right elements in the Rhodesian lobby is an adaptation of the domino theory which was popular during the Eisenhower administration as a rationale for U.S. policy in Southeast Asia. It helps to explain why the small band of 224,000 Rhodesian whites—no larger than any one of a number of English midland towns—should be given more attention at the moment than the 3,400,000 whites of South Africa. Dozens of domino variations have appeared in the extremist press since Rhodesia's Unilateral Declaration of Independence. In the version used in a "Dear Friend" letter sent out by the American "Friends of Rhodesian Independence," piquantly datelined "Washington's Birthday, 1966":

Rhodesia is the key to the West's precarious position in the Afro-Asian world. If Rhodesia falls, both South Africa and Portuguese Africa will inevitably follow like dominoes, leaving the entire continent in anti-Western hands. . . . *We must not allow this to happen.*

And as echoed by Congressman Joe D. Waggoner, Jr., Democrat of Louisiana, on April 5, 1966, on the floor of the United States House of Representatives:

The fact is that Rhodesia has become the cornerstone of this nation's tenuous foothold in the entire Afro-Asian world. If we are successful in our treacherous subversion of Rhodesia, there is no possibility that Portuguese Africa and South Africa can stand. When they, too, collapse, we will have no friend on the continent.

The implication of the domino theory that black Africans are our "enemies" and that the white ruling elites are our "friends" is naïve, and the view that the white redoubt is a strong anti-Communist bastion of the Western world is a dangerous fantasy. In fact, as an Afrikaner M.P. in the United Party told the South African Parliament on March 6, 1964, "Our government's racism is giving Communism the greatest opening it ever had in Africa."

American conservatives are correct in seeing a relationship between the Rhodesian, Portuguese African, and South African questions, but the domino theory is wrong in its assumption that the fall of the Smith government would lead to the fall of white-dominated governments in the other countries of southern Africa. White power would remain intact in South Africa, and Rhodesia under African majority rule would probably find it necessary to be as circumspect in its relations with South Africa as its neighbors do. Rather than take the dangerous step of becoming an active sanctuary for sabotage and terrorism against South Africa, Rhodesia might well exercise a constructive influence by demonstrating, as Kenya is doing, that a multiracial society under majority rule can work successfully without destroying the whites.

INTERESTS OF THE GREAT POWERS

With this background of southern African trends in mind, let us now examine their implications for the foreign policy of the United States. First, how important is the area to our national interest?

In general, the continent of Africa is less important to the United States than Europe, Asia, or Latin America. At times, however, as in the Congo crisis, and possibly in southern Africa in the future, it can rise to the top level of urgent problems. Today's interventionists, however, are attempting the apparently impossible task of persuading the world to deal with a problem before it becomes a crisis.

The strategic interests of the United States in southern Africa are of only minor importance to our security. We do have a substantial interest, however, in the availability of the naval base at Simonstown and the general importance of South Africa's location along sea lanes, especially when the Suez Canal route to the East is closed. Simonstown's naval repair installations are the only such facilities within more than 5000 miles and could be important in time of war. Our space tracking stations in South Africa are also useful, although we could get along without them.

Our economic interest in southern Africa is also of little direct importance to the United States, but significant for the American businesses involved. Of about $700 million in private investment in South Africa, $528 million is direct investment and the remainder portfolio investment. In the rest of southern Africa in mid-1967,

Americans had $56 million invested in Rhodesia, $50 million in Angola (mostly petroleum), and $25 million in Mozambique. As far as our trade with Africa is concerned, it is still true, as economist Andrew M. Kamarck wrote in 1958, that "we could get along without African commodities and African markets with an imperceptible ripple in our standard of living." It should be added, however, that in the future Africa will be more important to the American economy because our need to import raw materials is growing.

Indirectly, moreover, Africa is economically significant to us because of its larger importance to Western Europe, where we have a huge investment in European recovery and prosperity. African copper and other products that go to Europe also interest us in another indirect way because they complement or compete with Latin American products and affect the ability of Latin American countries to buy United States goods.

The greatest interest of the United States in southern Africa is clearly a political interest in fostering the kind of balance between freedom and stability that satisfies men's needs and enables them to work toward the attainment of their aspirations. The fact that we cannot be certain our efforts will succeed should not deter us from making the attempt.

Because of its limited interests in Africa, the policies of the United States government have traditionally been expressed in verbal generalities and in votes for U.N. resolutions condemning such things as apartheid in South Africa and the white seizure of power in Rhodesia. Privately, many of our diplomats have also done what they could to persuade the whites of southern Africa to change their policies, but such pleas have had little effect.

Verbal condemnations do, however, have some utility. They at least place the United States on public record in support of its oft-stated principles. In addition, they point up problems likely to arise in the future. As Assistant Secretary Palmer said in his Rhodesian policy statement of February 28, 1967:

The situation in Southern Rhodesia . . . has already served to heighten racial tensions in and around Rhodesia itself . . . [it] could serve to consolidate and extend the strength and attitudes of white supremacists in Southern Africa. The result of such a continued polarization in Africa of extremist racial philosophies can only be instability, strife and chaos.

Unlike the Western countries, the Communist states have never held colonies in Africa, have never invested in the continent, and have never had significant trade relations with the African states. Though the defense of economic interests partly explains Western policy in Africa, this is not the case with the Communist countries.

Political factors are dominant in the relations of Communist states with Africa. This has been true for a number of reasons, some internal to Communist philosophy, some related to pride in non-Western solidarity, and some related to the configuration of power and alliances in international politics since World War II.

Since World War II the United States has attempted to contain the expansion of Communism by alliances, base agreements, and military assistance to countries on the periphery of the Soviet Union, Eastern Europe, and China. However, after a short-lived inclination to regard neutralism as immoral, both the United States and the Soviet Union now seem content to keep Africa out of the camp of the other.

The late 1950s and early 1960s was a period of considerable Soviet-American competition in aid to the many fledgling states of Africa. In December, 1960, the director of the Agency for International Development declared that foreign aid was "the most effective arsenal we have in the cold war." It was not long, however, before setbacks came to both the Soviet and the American efforts to influence African policy through aid. The informal détente between the United States and the Soviet Union in other spheres began to affect their African policies as both countries sought to reduce or level off their aid commitments. Meanwhile Americans were expressing exaggerated concern over a mounting Communist Chinese threat to Africa or, as Africans say, a Chinese threat to the United States in Africa. Excluded from the United Nations and other forums of international diplomacy, China helped to create its own forums such as the Afro-Asian People's Solidarity Organization and other bodies through which China could influence Africans. But China's militant revolutionary appeal to peoples over the heads of their governments soon produced an inevitable reaction, and several African leaders broke diplomatic relations with Peking. China's conflict with the Soviet Union also weakened Chinese influence because Africans seek to steer clear of the rivalries of the great powers.

By 1967, many observers were exaggerating the failures of the Chinese in Africa almost as much as they exaggerated their successes four years earlier. It must not be forgotten that the racial attitudes of the white supremacists throughout southern Africa produce African reactions that are made to order for permanent Chinese exploitation. It should be added that this is also true of the Russians who, despite the Soviet-American détente, could escalate a crisis in southern Africa in the future, just as they tried to do in the Arab-Israeli war in 1967.

IMPLICATIONS FOR AMERICAN POLICY

For American policy, the implications of the foregoing observations are clear. It is indispensable to continue both persuasion and pressure on the right-wing governments of South Africa, Portugal, and Rhodesia to change the direction of their policies. This does not necessarily mean the use of force. The United States does not want any more wars. It has too many already. There is no disposition in the government of either the United States or the United Kingdom to engage in large-scale economic sanctions backed by a naval blockade of South Africa. The possibility remains, however, no matter how remote it seems at present, that widespread racial conflict would drag the great powers into southern Africa.

If peaceful progress is to be made in southern Africa, it must come step by step. In mid-1967 the key issue in the white redoubt was Rhodesia. The United Kingdom made a commitment to the Commonwealth prime ministers that it will adhere to the principle of "no independence before majority rule" (NIBMAR). At the same time, Britain is trying to decolonize, and there is considerable opposition to "going back into the colonial business." The U.K. is also predominantly concerned with moving into the European Economic Community. It would not be surprising, therefore, if the Wilson government tries to negotiate a settlement short of NIB-

MAR, granting independence with some type of guarantee for ultimate majority rule. We have seen, however, that the present illegal
government of Rhodesia is composed of politicians who have a long
record of fighting progress toward majority rule, and it is therefore
reasonable to assume that if they obtain their independence, they
will try to evade any such commitments or guarantees. A violation
of the NIBMAR principle is therefore likely to lead to a prolonged
period of instability in central and southern Africa, and the possible
withdrawal of Zambia and other countries from the Commonwealth. It would also undermine the position of whites in other
parts of the continent, notably in Kenya where relations between
black and white are still good. Conversely, the whites of Rhodesia
should fare reasonably well under majority rule. Their technical
and administrative skills would still be needed and they would still
have the power and the moral and economic support of South African whites behind them. No doubt they would have difficulties under majority rule, but the alternative of trying to enforce minority
rule will lead sooner or later to even more trouble.

As for South Africa, the economic and political reasons why
apartheid cannot solve South Africa's problems have been made
quite clear by South African economist Desmond Hobart Houghton
and numerous other South African scholars. Whites need and want
African laborers in the white areas, and no government could sur-
vive a real attempt to remove them. Moreover, even if all Africans
could be removed from white areas to the reserves, the reserves
could not support them. The reserves have virtually no capital, limited raw materials, and very few industrial markets because of lack
of buying power. Instead of allowing white capital to develop the
reserves, the government's alternative is to locate industries on the
South African side of the border where they would utilize labor
from the reserves or "Bantu homelands" during the daytime. This is
hardly calculated to allow Africans to "rise to the top in their own
sphere," the alleged objective of apartheid.

The government has no intention of removing the African labor
force from the white areas. It seeks to send back to the reserves
those who can be dispensed with, but to transform most workers
into a vast labor pool of transients with no political rights in the

white area. This exposes another basic flaw in the theory of apartheid, for there would always be more blacks than whites in the
"white" area, and the proportion of Africans is increasing. In the attempt to get around this inconsistency, the government gives Africans in the white areas the right to cast absentee ballots in elections
for limited self-government in their "homelands." Or at least this is
true in the Transkei, the only Bantustan thus far created. It is inconceivable that this fanciful idea will satisfy the demand of urban
Africans for political rights. In fact, and this is the heart of the matter, the whole concept of apartheid is politically unrealistic because
it is solely a white man's idea, adopted without true consultation
with the African people, in an age of self-determination when black
men everywhere seek a voice in shaping their own destiny. Apartheid can be maintained for a time, but only by force.

The dilemma of South Africa's whites is indeed a difficult one,
but in the end they will have to devise a policy that is based on
consent rather than force. This means that, if they want to continue
the present integration of about 60 percent of the African population in the white economy, they ultimately will have to give non-
whites in the white area the political rights commensurate with
their economic status. The much publicized "flexibility" and "pragmatism" of Prime Minister B. J. Vorster have not in any way even
approached this fundamental problem. His steps to alleviate some
of the absurdities of "petty apartheid" are most welcome, but the
United States should continue to press South Africans to come to
grips with the real issue.

In thinking about the future, it is important to avoid succumbing
to two fallacies that are being currently advocated by opponents of
pressure. The first is the contention that pressure should be relaxed
because it only rigidifies and solidifies the whites in their defiance;
the second is the wishful thought that, if pressure is relaxed, economic integration will kill apartheid.

The view that pressure only rigidifies the whites overlooks the
fact that, after their initial gestures of defiance, South Africans
compensate in other ways. The enormous effort of the Information
Service to justify apartheid to the outside world is one kind of compensation, and it has unintended effects by inducing South Africans

to clarify their thinking and gradually to discard outmoded concepts. The invention of the Bantustan plan was in part a response to external demands that Africans be given the right to vote. The Odendaal Plan for South West Africa and the relative speed with which it was completed was still another response to pressure. Moreover, the fallacy in the argument that external pressures only unite South Africans in resisting change becomes even clearer when one recognizes that it applies to the less than 20 percent of the people who are white. For the whites know that they have to live with the African, Coloured, and Indian peoples, who are emboldened by external support. This knowledge is in itself another kind of pressure. As a South African sociologist, Leo Kuper, writes in his book, *An African Bourgeoisie:* "The granitelike commitment to apartheid cannot be taken for granted." Apartheid theorists have already moved from "white domination" to "separate development" and now on to "self-government." Moreover, some of the cabinet ministers have repeatedly warned their followers that "you can't keep the black man down." The pressure to develop a more workable policy will mount as the failure of apartheid becomes more widely recognized.

The second fallacy is a kind of "hormone weed-killer" theory that rapid growth and the accompanying integration of Africans into the modern economy will kill apartheid and solve the problem of race relations. In this view, which has understandably attained a certain popularity in business circles, Americans can help to kill apartheid by increasing their investment in South Africa's economic growth. Ironically, there has been enough talk along these lines to stimulate South Africans to make a number of public statements warning American business against such motives.

The fallacy in the idea that industrialization will upset the established order of race relations is clearly demonstrated in a 1965 study of *Industrialization and Race Relations,* edited by Guy Hunter. Sponsored by UNESCO and the Institute of Race Relations in London, this symposium compares the effect of industrialization on race relations in many countries, and, in Hunter's words, "confirms overwhelmingly the subservience of the industrial to the racial pattern." Although it seems logical to expect that the contacts, effi-

ciency, mobility, and secularism of industry would modify the racial pattern, the fact is that the deep-seated passions behind the
racial order in societies such as South Africa and the American South
act "so powerfully upon the industrializing process that the pull of
its gravity is largely counteracted." Industrialization adjusts, adapts,
and accommodates itself to the racial mold. The racial pattern in
the United States is changing not because of industrialization but
because of the effects of Federal political action and of politically
inspired economic action." The effects of industrialization on a rigid
racial pattern are only marginal and indirect; to the extent that it
results in economic advancement it makes Africans more conscious
of their capacity to advance and therefore may lead them to try to
step up their political action to end racial discrimination.

Let us not allow the power of the whites in southern Africa to
blind us to the fact that relaxation of pressure for a change of policy would be counterproductive. It would only further the belief,
already heard from South Africans and Rhodesians, that the West
is beginning to recognize the justice and wisdom of their positions.
It would also undermine the credibility of American denunciations
of racial discrimination. It would tend to polarize conflict along racial lines by giving Africans the feeling that the whites of the world
were uniting against them. It would be injurious to our political,
economic, and strategic interests in the rest of Africa and the non-
white world. And it would further undermine our interests in the
United Nations.

No doubt the struggle for peaceful change in southern Africa will
be a long one with many disappointments, and it may fail in the
end. But the United States has nothing to gain by abandoning its
insistence on the basic principles that just governments should be
based on the consent of the governed, and that we oppose all laws
that discriminate against a human being because of the color of his
skin.

New White Politics
in South Africa

-≺☼≻-

Edwin S. Munger

THE THRUST of this chapter would have been quite different if it had been written at the conclusion of World War II. Indeed, until the 1961 republican referendum, the emphasis would have focused on domestic politics centering around the almost wholly Afrikaner National Party and the largely English-speaking United Party, with some reference to the Progressive and Liberal parties.

By 1967, however, white versus white domestic politics had been replaced by two new trends, developing in the last years of the Verwoerdian era and accelerated with the advent of Prime Minister Vorster. First of these has been the unification of the white oligarchy. The most significant of the many factors responsible for the emergence of this trend have been violence, the growing number of English-speaking Nationalists, the rise of black voices, the extent of urbanization in South Africa which has turned many Afrikaans-speaking farmers' sons into industrial workers, and the ascendance of Afrikaner businessmen to rival the politicians and *predikante* (clergymen). White acceptance of political decentralization, that is, the granting of some measure of autonomy to certain Bantu areas, has occurred concurrently with a centralization of white politics at the expense of provincial party politics. The election of Capetonian Dr. Eben Dönges as state president in 1967, when the Transvaalers held the National Party votes, is symbolic of this decline in regionalism.

The decline in distrust between English and Afrikaner is a phenomenon of the last few years. It has been well said in South Africa that coalition in the 1930s did not work because just as General Hertzog kept looking back to see if the Afrikaners were with him, so General Smuts did the same to be sure that the English-speaking South Africans remained behind him. The result was that the English distrusted Hertzog and the Afrikaners referred to "slim [clever, unreliable] Jannie Smuts."

Smuts had lifted a bitter pen for the Afrikaners with his "A Century of Wrong" indictment of Great Britain in the Boer War period, but what followed was a half century of mistrust. Although such mistrust does not disappear overnight, for a great majority of English- and Afrikaans-speaking whites there has been a notable mellowing of old antipathies.

The second trend in the transformation of white political thinking has been the shift from essentially domestic issues to foreign affairs. This is, of course, a reflection of growing international pressure arising out of widespread feeling in the world that white South Africa suppresses black South Africa. One could have forecast this almost twenty years ago when, in 1948, the Afrikaner Nationalists came to power with the slogan "apartheid," promising but not immediately providing a solution to racial problems which had existed almost from the day that Jan van Riebeeck landed at the Cape in 1652. It was not until 1966–67 that the foreign repercussions to these problems caused a profound reaction on the South African political scene and gave a sharp political edge to foreign affairs debates in Parliament. Previously, isolated voices had referred to Africa north of the Limpopo, but the first organized South African diplomatic offensive in Africa, beyond its own borders, did not begin in earnest until 1967. Many popular American and British publications "discovered" a domestic dialogue as well as a change in external South African politics. For example, a lead article in *The Reporter* (May 4, 1967) began: "South Africa, after nineteen years of isolation from the rest of the world and studied defiance of it, has initiated a sudden and dramatic change of policy." It is all very well for the author, Noel Mostert, to speak of "startling initiatives" but quite shallow of him to proclaim that "all this represents the

first hint of any change whatsoever . . . since the Nationalists
came to power in 1948." New plants grow from seeds, and one objective of this chapter is to do more than recognize the flowering—
which may or may not be as ephemeral as that of Namaqualand
daisies. It is to dig down and examine the roots.

UNIFICATION OF THE WHITE OLIGARCHY

Our first major concern is marked by the shift from a period of several decades—during which white parties debated *each other* concerning what to do about the Bantu, the Coloured, and the
Indians—to the present, when the debate/struggle primarily involves the white parties on the one hand and the non-white groups
on the other, with most of the world siding with the majority.

Emergence of the African Presence

Let there be no mistake: South African white politics always
have been about white-black relations. There were differences on
policy underlying the Great Trek of 1836 as well as the establishment of the South African Republic and the Orange Free State,
which had joined together during the Boer War (the Second War
for South African Independence). However, a debate between two
white groups concerning the status of a black group is fundamen-
tally different from the present situation where a united white
group engages in struggle or dialogue with a black group or
groups.

It may seem inappropriate to refer to a "dialogue" when, in fact,
at this juncture of South African history there exists in the country
an even greater polarization of white and black than at any previous period. In the strictly political environment the personal contacts perhaps are fewer than they have been for forty years. There
is less general dialogue about the racial future between whites and
Africans. But then originally much of this dialogue was paternal-
istic, condescending, and rooted in basic assumptions of biological
inferiority. New discussions between Africans who are members of
urban advisory boards or officers of actual and potential Bantustans

and Afrikaners are more genuine than any which have taken place since the Voortrekkers parleyed with African chiefs. Thus the sense in which "dialogue" is of critical importance lies in the fact that white and black groups now are facing each other without intermediate translators inside South Africa. There are, of course, even more intensive discussions at the far left, many of them outside South Africa.

In South Africa the day of the white man speaking for the black man is over. This fundamental fact has had extensive repercussions in many spheres of black-white relations. It underlay the rise of the Pan-Africanist Congress when it challenged, among other practices, the white Communist domination of the African National Congress. The failure of the nonracial, but white-led, Liberal Party to gain a significant following among Africans may be attributed to it. As a direct consequence of this development the authority of white officials to speak for Africans over whom they have control has been diminished. Now, when the man in charge of African affairs in Pretoria city wants to introduce change—birth control pills were a 1967 example—he asks prominent Africans for their advice—and not as Uncle Toms or in a condescending manner. It is sometimes thought that the African staff of the new university colleges are spinelessly subservient to their white principals. However, those white principals who are not genuinely sympathetic to some African aspirations and prepared to battle for them, and who do not rely heavily upon the advice and wisdom of their African staff, have experienced nothing but trouble.

Businessmen, often the last group to be politically sensitive, for some years now have been calling for African unions with African leadership in an effort to achieve a direct dialogue between management and labor. Although unions are still technically illegal, many African organizations do, in fact, function as such.

Paradoxical or not, the movement in the United States whereby Negroes rather than whites speak for Negroes in the North or the South has coincided with the end of the period in South Africa when white men speak for Africans. In both countries this has resulted in the feelings of some white liberals being hurt, and even has led to occasional charges of anti-Semitism against the new black leadership.

White parties and, indeed, the white Parliament have been demoted from being the final judges in decision making. Now Parliament determines what the white *view* will be. While this view is backed by the state, it is not omnipotent. Based upon long-held Afrikaner convictions about the value of instruction in the mother tongue—convictions with considerable scientific validity in other parts of the world where race is not an issue—the white position has been, and remains for most of the Republic, that Africans should not begin to learn English before acquiring thorough mastery of their tribal language. The United Party opposition to this policy has been outvoted repeatedly by the swelling majorities of the National Party. In a sense the white Parliament's decision on the primacy of the mother tongue was only the penultimate one; the final verdict of the all-African legislature in the Transkei was to act against the wishes of the whites by following Xhosa language teaching with English (not Afrikaans) at an early age. This is now the practice. In another recent instance, Transkeian Prime Minister K. D. Matanzima, whose territory will be financially dependent on South Africa for many years to come, still had sufficient political muscle to visit Cape Town, argue with white cabinet ministers, and succeed in obtaining the release of a man (a teacher, subsequently appointed minister of education in the Transkei) banned under the ubiquitous Suppression of Communism Act.[1]

It is because the African voice is being heard now that, while white-black relations were never more important, white politics per se no longer tell the full story. White leadership in the Communist Party, in the Nederduits Gereformeerde Church, in the running of

[1] Both the Transkei and the "Ovambostan" in South West Africa are known popularly as Bantustans. The South African government prefers to speak of "homelands" under a policy of "separate development." This paper uses "Bantustans" without any pejorative intent, although the Asian derivation is obvious. Today, the Bantustans perhaps most resemble Uzbekistan, Turkmenistan, and Kazakhstan in having a certain cultural autonomy but far from absolute political control on major issues coming from Pretoria or Moscow. The model of Pakistan carries a concept of partition, a subject often bruited in South Africa. Finally, Afghanistan as an independent state is another mode. The destiny of "Bantustans" is as yet uncertain.

African townships, and even in businesses is being challenged and is willingly giving ground to some African participation in decision making. The degree of participation varies widely. The election of Seth Mokitimi as head of the South African Methodist Church (for white and black) represents major participation. In the Nederduits Gereformeerde Church, it is much less, although titles for Bantu clergy have been brought into line with those for white clergy. Recently, a delegation of Dutch Reformed ministers visiting the Netherlands included an African minister who argued against the Dutch criticism of the South African churches. The considerable growth in the buying power of the increasingly urbanized Bantu population is a particularly important factor domestically, responsible for compelling the whites to regard Africans not only as workers but also as consumers. Africans have a measurably greater potential economic strength to disrupt South Africa—but much less political or military ability to apply it—than they had in the turbulent 1950s.

The emergence of a new kind of black voice to which whites could listen does not necessarily mean that significant internal change is on the horizon. The very recognition by whites of a potential African threat to their pleasant *status quo* may have fostered an illusion that not only is it acceptable for Africans to have views on the general society but that they actually are listened to by whites. African economic improvement may provide a speaking platform, but this is no guarantee that white society will listen except at its own choice. And there is no doubt that white recognition of potential African strength has contributed to white unification.

The Resort to Violence

Organized attack against the government has been limited in South Africa since the end of the "Kaffir" Wars. When it has occurred, there has been a tacit understanding that it stemmed from political differences and did not involve "civilians." The Jameson Raid, *Die Rebellie* of the die-hard Afrikaners in 1914, and the occasional efforts at sabotage by Afrikaner groups in the early years of World War II were not directed at killing people. While government reprisals have been fierce—most notably by the Smuts gov-

ernment in such incidents as the Bondelswart Rebellion of 1922—
arrested individuals usually have been let off relatively lightly, be
they English, Afrikaner, or African. It is highly unlikely that the
death sentence would have been imposed even if the famous "Trea-
son Trial" of 1956–61 had ended in convictions.

Much of the support which the various leaders of the African National Congress and other African groupings derived from the
white, middle-class, English-speaking section of South Africa in the
three decades from 1930 to 1960 was due to an emphasis upon
words rather than bullets. Toward the end of this period, a frequent focus for discussion among antigovernment groups was
whether sabotage involving people would alienate more potential
white friends than it would encourage Africans and create situations in which government reprisals would bring world sympathy.
The Communist Party wrestled with this issue for a long time. The
first step—that of sabotage without loss of life—had a brief vogue.
It usually failed to achieve its goals and was counter-productive in
gradually increasing police efficiency, low at the beginning of the
period, and in securing more financial support for police training
and equipment.

South Africa has lived with a high rate of lawlessness for the last
three centuries. Now it is directed mainly by Africans against Africans—a major reason the white oligarchy has taken so little action. For the whites, robberies and burglaries in such centers as
Johannesburg are a tolerable evil, involving the hiring of night
watchmen or filling out insurance claim forms. It still is revealing to
thumb through the advertising pages of the Johannesburg telephone directory and see the range of elaborate defenses offered
against burglars. The artistic steel latticework guarding windows in
most white homes gives validity to the observation that the white
man sleeps behind the bars of the black man's zoo.

But neither the bloody scenes at non-white hospital emergency
rooms after the annual Christmas Eve knifings, nor the intricate
alarm systems on windows, were a significant force in the unification of the white oligarchy. African violence against African did
not arouse whites; it even appeared to confirm some of the white
stereotypes.

The 1964 Johannesburg Station bombing, in which an elderly woman died, her granddaughter was severely burned, and tens of commuters were injured, was a turning point in white public opinion. Hitherto, long and sometimes acrimonious debates accompanied steps to strengthen the police or enlarge the army. Many whites in opposition to the government felt the answer was racial justice—not more arrests. However, the station bombing, having as its objective the killing of dozens of white people (whatever their political views) as they rushed for trains, combined with train derailments and other sabotage efforts deliberately directed at killing, produced a continuing white backlash. Most of the organization of sabotage and many of its successes have been achieved by white-dominated groups. Some of them have been led by Communists, others by non-Communists of strongly liberal persuasion. The greatest police efforts were directed against the white leadership of the Communist Party, ARM (the predominantly white "African Resistance Movement"), etc. Despite the coloration of the leadership, however, it was the African "cause" that lay at the heart of the bombings. Violence erupting in this guise did succeed in uniting the white oligarchy. Those who aimed to kill succeeded in attracting attention. As they feared, they unified the whites, but whatever "inspiration" they may have given to some African elements was short-lived.

While the Progressive Party never for a moment condoned such violence (the Liberal Party did not either, but a few members resigned one week and undertook violence the next), the cause of the Progressives suffered, just as it had suffered in South Africa when headlines of the first Congo upheavals influenced voters and appeared to give credence to National Party *swart gevaar* (black danger) electioneering.

It is the view of hundreds of thousands of white South Africans that (1) Africans have just grievances against society and (2) that the government must be strongly supported to prevent any violence dedicated to promoting change. From abroad, this juxtaposition of sentiments may appear irrational. Fear does produce irrationality, especially fear of the unknown. Many whites would support change, but change to and for what? The blueprints for the future,

in the ken of many ordinary white South Africans, have been obscured by the smoke of sabotage. These whites usually recognize
that the available channels through which the Africans might re-
dress their grievances are either blocked or opened only along a
few avenues carefully chosen by the government. In party politics,
the United Party has had little alternative but to stand behind the
National Party government. For a while, the United Party could
add to its shock at violence the position "but it is partly the government's fault." Today, this argument carries little weight with the
majority of whites. What does count is that by whatever Draconian
laws—justified by most whites as forced upon the government by
unusual circumstances—the measures of the National Party government have been remarkably effective in decreasing the extent of
sabotage of property and loss of life. The risk of escalation to
which the revolutionary whites and Africans finally resorted after
decades of indecision has not paid off. Furthermore, the Commu-
nist-led efforts, such as those so fully revealed by the Rivonia Farm
raid of July, 1963, and in the activities of Communist leader Braam
Fischer before his capture, pulled the legs from beneath many English-speaking whites who sincerely had defended Fischer and his
colleagues as not being Communists but persecuted liberals.
Fischer's dramatic affirmation of his long devotion to the Communist cause and his espousal of violence further undermined non-
Communist opposition to unification of the white oligarchy. In the
end, efforts to create chaos or fear have been successfully countered
by the government, violence has ebbed, fear has declined, and the
government has been strengthened in its views that might must be
white.

Industrialization and White Politics

Urbanization and associated problems have been a dynamic
force in South Africa almost as far back as Union. Striking African
latrine workers "downed buckets" in 1918 for a mere sixpence a day
more from the municipality. The "battle of Witwatersrand," which
raged in 1922, pitted the white workers against their bosses. For a
long time the National Party was able to solidify its Afrikaner sup-

porters backing them against the "English" industrialists. A present
cabinet minister, Albert Hertzog, long advocated nationalization of
the gold mines. The Afrikaners were the radicals; the English the
conservative owners of the biggest farms and the factories. There
was also a touch of anti-Semitism. The "Hoggenheimer" cartoons
of *Die Burger* reflected anti-Semitism, as well as the farmer's distrust of the rich mortgage owner.

This era has all but vanished in the dynamic changes which followed World War II. Most Afrikaners now live in cities. The National Party has stormed one United Party urban stronghold after
another. In succession, solidly United Party towns along the Rand
have succumbed; first to fall were Boksburg, Germiston, and farther off Vereeninging, and then in 1966 such towns as Benoni (at
one time a strong Labor seat) and Springs. All are now in Nationalist hands. No longer are one quarter of the Afrikaners poor whites
who must be subsidized (at the expense of African jobs) with pick-
and-shovel work on the railroads. Afrikaner insurance companies
have grown strong. The most dynamic bank in South Africa is not
found among the English-oriented Barclays or Standard or even the
Volkskas, organized with such fervor by Afrikaners in the Transvaal, but is Jan Marais' Cape-based Trust Bank, which features
beautiful girls and which pioneers with more convenient hours and
customer services.

Afrikaners now buy common stocks where once they would buy
only land. With both astuteness and political muscle they have entered one "English" preserve after another. Coal, diamonds, clothing manufacture, the list is a long and impressive one. The day is
past when the response of "English" South Africa was to place a
"tame" Afrikaner on the board of directors. Now the deal is direct
and between business equals, albeit the English establishment still
maintains a preponderance of power. What is more significant is
that in one venture after another the whole concept of "power
fight" has been succeeded by partnership. In South Africa today,
most new industrial enterprises include both Afrikaner and English
companies—and each with shareholders of the opposite language
group. Symbolic of the new pattern are the "deals" involving
Oppenheimer's Anglo-American Corporation and Afrikaner capi-

talists. Such a traditional "English" corporation as General Mining was taken over by Federale Mynbou in one of the more dramatic changes.

These mergers and partnerships occasionally are attacked in the right-wing Afrikaans press, which grew up thinking of business as evil and English. Today, Afrikaner critics cannot aim many darts at the "bosses" without hitting a fellow Afrikaner with the power to retaliate.

The political significance of the rise of Afrikaner business rests upon the fact that an Afrikaner government is not unhappy to be in partnership with business. Conversely, business has a leverage on government which it did not have when the National Party first came to power in 1948. Whatever the Finance Minister does about import controls affects Afrikaner and English businessmen. There is a common concern with the economic prosperity of the Republic. This concern is discussed in the Prime Minister's economic advisory council, a body which includes among its members academic economists, Jewish businessmen, and men with Progressive Party views on racial affairs. All this would have been inconceivable in the 1948 model of the National Party.

Up until 1960, members of certain non-Afrikaner groups would neither have been asked nor have accepted the invitation to advise on economic matters. The change has occurred from both sides.

To appreciate the new role of Afrikaner businessmen, one must recall that the early leadership of Afrikaner nationalism relied heavily upon ministers of religion. In many nineteenth-century Afrikaans communities, the leaders were the Scots Presbyterian ministers. Dr. Malan was first a minister, then editor of *Die Burger* when it was founded, and later prime minister. For a long period Afrikaner leadership was strongly dependent upon *predikante* and politicians. In the 1948 and 1953 elections, the United Party charged that it was impossible to distinguish one role from the other.

Today, Afrikaner businessmen are often nonpolitical but, nonetheless, influential within the Afrikaner hierarchy. Their own welfare depends on the welfare of South Africa; they distrust political ideology, which they judge will breed internal or external trouble.

This may include ideas of Afrikaner politicians. The commitment of Afrikaner businessmen to a "separate development" is as strong or stronger than that of the wealthy farmers. Yet they are usually far more enlightened on matters of race. They will complain, for example, against "little apartheid" for its pettiness and individual human suffering. Like their conservative "English" business colleagues, they are against "agitators," but at the same time they oppose too many laws detailing the lives of men. The unification of the white oligarchy has been solidified by the emergence of Afrikaner business.

There is another significant aspect to the rise of Afrikaner businessmen and their close relations with the "English" section. This lies in a broadly similar approach to African labor. The Bantu Wage and Productivity Association was originally "English," but its influence has become widespread among all white employers in raising wages of non-white employees. A decade ago, neither English nor Afrikaner businessmen paid much attention to good race relations as a matter of company policy. Now the leading companies regularly send their managers into the classroom to learn how to gain a deeper insight into the nature of the total labor force. Courses include such familiar subjects as courtesy and good manners toward people of all races, and a particular appreciation of the traditional milieu out of which most African workers have come.

The white business community has advanced toward a recognition that it is not enough to pay Africans higher wages than are paid in ex-colonial African countries. The standards by which South African wages often are judged and found to be lacking are not those of the poorer African countries but of the affluent European ones. On the other hand, the disparity between wages of white and black people far outweighs the differences in educational opportunity and subsequent skills. Although African wages have increased, it is not easy to ascertain from the limited available studies to what extent they have risen relative to living costs. Professor Hance's chapter sheds some light on this topic. While it notes that over five and a half years there has been an increase of 45 percent in African manufacturing wages as compared with a rise of only 14 percent in the cost of living, the figures can be deceptive in con-

cealing much individual hardship, as is suggested by the data from
cost-of-living studies.

The official "suspension" or, more often, the ignoring of "job
reservation" is no more English than Afrikaner. Afrikaner businessmen "bootleg" skilled African labor and pay bonuses to meet
the same economic goals as their fellow businessmen. The number
of Africans who are paid the *same* wages for the *same* work has
grown rapidly in South Africa, but quantitative data are difficult to
obtain. Leading the field in this approach of "equal pay for equal
work as long as the fact is not known" are the government-run railways and defense plants.

The relevant point here is the new-found recognition within the
business community of a situation that for so long was ignored but
which now is in the limelight. Thus, the whites' growing political,
human, and economic consciousness of the African's position in society is yet another factor contributing to the unification of the
white oligarchy.

All of this represents a by-product of industrialization and attests
to the termination of the simple dichotomy of English businessman
vs. Afrikaner farmer. Most of the forces working to improve the
economic lot of Africans in South Africa are not motivated by political idealism or human compassion; it is simply that South Africa is
being rapidly modernized in such a way that the whites are drawn
together—but not against Africans in an economic sense. For Africans also are being drawn toward the unified whites. When an Afrikaner girl operates a machine by day and an African man operates
the same machine by night—as in some factories, with the salary
difference being the bonus for night work—then the economic unification embraces more than the whites alone.

The Growth of "English" Nationalists

Two decades ago Afrikaner families seeking refuge from the win-
try veld and towns of the Transvaal and Orange Free State in the
warm sun of Natal's South Coast found signs in English only. Durban shopgirls were not only rude but responded only in English.
To most English in Natal, the idea of being a Nationalist in Natal

(save the northern seats) was like being an anarchist—the bloody Nats (or "Natzis") were ruining the country. A decade ago the rebellion of English-speaking Natal against Afrikanerdom was manifested by the grass-roots support of the Federal Party; secession of the province was debated over many a gin and bitters.

Durban, it is true, was the first South African city to endorse Group Areas. The concept had its origins in the Pegging Act supported by Smuts and was designed to keep Durban Indians from expanding into "white areas." Liberal Natalians despised the National Party for endorsing Group Areas, while the supporters of the United Party, as city councilors, embraced the concept. The parliamentary support which the Progressives enjoyed in their initial breakaway from the United Party came from these liberals. The conservative, anti-Indian Natalian of the "English" establishment, on the other hand, had no use for the upstart Nationalists; children were even shut up if they used a word of Afrikaans, although by law the children studied it in school. In fact, if a few years ago the Administrator of Natal had approved the recent appointment of two Indians and one European as the first multiracial town board for deciding on trade licenses, the anti-Afrikaans feeling would have equaled the anti-Indian feeling.

It can readily be posited that it was the existence among traditional Natalians of a basic bigotry and a desire for authoritarian control of the "Indians and Kaffirs" which provided susceptible material for National Party recruitment. But this would be an oversimplification. Natal has changed; it has become *tweetalig* (bilingual). This new trend received an impetus from the inclusion of English-speaking whites in Verwoerd's cabinet. In recent years, through the brilliant leadership of Theo Gerdener, the government-appointed administrator, many of the grievances of Natalians have been resolved. The white Natalian exception to Nationalist isolation has been met by the greater concern for foreign affairs. Even when the "Nats" were most unpopular, Foreign Minister Eric Louw was enthusiastically received in Durban after returning from the United Nations.

A striking indication of the marked shift in Natalian attitudes is to be found in the efforts of Stellenbosch University to raise money in Natal Province. Stellenbosch in the Western Cape not only is the epitome of Afrikaner tradition but is naturally a rival of the University of Natal. A decade ago, it would have been fortunate to raise $10,000 from the "English" community of Durban and Natal. However, with a committee of twelve prominent Natal businessmen, of whom all but one were "English" and not previously associated with Stellenbosch, the Afrikaans university raised almost a quarter of a million dollars.

That the donations carried strong political overtones together with a desire to help a specifically Afrikaans institution was highlighted later on during the University of Cape Town's (English medium) far less successful fund-raising campaign in Natal.

Support for the National Party has also grown among English-speaking Transvaalers. Here, however, it has created a problem for the Nationalists. In Natal, the Nationalist branches spoke English and had English-speaking leadership. In the Transvaal, the practice had been to group right-wing English-speaking Nationalists into one party branch. This was acceptable for a while. Many of these people were European, often from Central Europe rather than from the United Kingdom, and they formed what was essentially a club in the John X. Merriman branch. When South African-born "English" whites began to be attracted to party branches, the Nationalists were faced with a dilemma which the party has yet to solve satisfactorily. With almost the entire branch being English in Natal, the language was English and there was no leadership division between English- and Afrikaans-speaking contestants. In the Transvaal, many Afrikaner party branches were reluctant to let their traditional "enemies" play an active role, speak English, or stand for party nomination.

In rural areas, Afrikaner Nationalists have dominated and continue to dominate organizations affecting youth. Most teachers of English in many parts of the *platteland* speak Afrikaans as their home language. Small wonder that the number of United Party supporters has shrunk and little headway has been made by the Progressives. Many Free Staters, of both language groups, feel that their province has suffered from lack of an opposition.

In the past the United Party unquestionably represented both language groups. The party which originated from both English and Afrikaner stock constituted an attempt to bring Afrikaner and English "moderates" together, excluding the pro-U.K. Dominion Party and the radical Afrikaners. The United Party probably still continues to attract more Afrikaner voters than the Nationalists gather "English" supporters. Nonetheless, the growth of "English" Nationalists is a strong contribution to unification of the white oligarchy. This reconciliation of English and Afrikaner has taken place against the backdrop of rising African demands for political rights. Although the African National Congress has been voicing demands since 1912, these were not seriously acknowledged by most whites until the Passive Defiance Campaign and similar political maneuvers of the 1950s.

Blurring of Provincial Differences

In discussing the change in Natal and the Afrikaner's new readiness to accept it as an integral part of South Africa, one must not overlook the declining individualism of other provinces. In party and national politics the numerical dominance of the Transvaal has all but ended the long struggle between the Cape Nationalists and the Transvaalers. The local opposition in Beaufort West (Cape Province) to the party nomination of Transvaaler Hilgard Muller as foreign minister may be cited as one of the many instances of strong party feeling at the provincial level. Another was the contest for succession to the office of prime minister following Strijdom, which went to a vote along provincial lines and for the first time in Nationalist Party history did not end in a unanimous vote.

To a certain extent the antagonism within the Nationalist hierarchy has derived from contrasting the political successes of the Afrikaners in the Transvaal with the equally great business successes of the Cape Afrikaners. Competition between the two most important provinces extends over many areas, including business, politics, sport, the creation and expansion of universities, etc. One instance of this is the fierce internal squabble in the Afrikaans press which resulted from the decision of *Die Nasionale Pers* (The National Press), in the Cape, to establish *Die Beeld* (The Image) as a new Sunday newspaper in Johannesburg. This followed the mass distribution of Johannesburg Sunday papers in Cape Town, Port Elizabeth, and their environs. Apparently the outcome of this dispute will be determined by economic considerations. Prime Minister Vorster, as chairman of the now combined northern publishing groups, including *Die Transvaler* (Verwoerd was the wartime editor) and *Die Vaderland* (the Afrikaner Party paper of General Hertzog), has remained above the tumult and has not exercised political advantage, a fact which reflects a closer relationship with the Cape Party than that enjoyed by Dr. Verwoerd.

Although the actual number of "English" who have "gone over" to an Afrikaner-led National Party is not large, there has been a noticeable shift in attitude among many of the United Party supporters, matching that voiced by the press and some United Party leaders. The most frequently mentioned factors marking this shift in "English" thinking are the Republic and Prime Minister Macmillan's "Winds of Change" speech, which *seemed* to say: for us in Great Britain you English are expendable.

In the past a philosophical difference was often cited as the reason for Transvaal vs. Cape antagonism. The Transvaal was pictured as being involved in the harsh black-white conflict in a pioneer environment. The image of the Cape as being older, more civilized, with a mellow moderation, and concerned with gradations between white and black—the Coloured people being the largest population group in Cape Town—certainly was true at one stage. Today, one cannot so easily characterize the views which a Transvaal Nationalist M.P. might have concerning Africans or Coloured people, as compared with those held by a Cape Nationalist. Differences in views persist, but far less along provincial lines.

Anti-Americanism, so much on the rise among white South Africans in recent years, has not been confined to a particular province. If feeling was stronger in the Transvaal, centered in the administrative capital of Pretoria, the whites in the Cape (and some sections of the Coloured community) reacted with considerable bitterness over the cancellation of shore leave for the crew of the aircraft carrier *Franklin D. Roosevelt* in 1966. The preparations in Cape Town to eliminate any residual ill feeling from the cancellation of the previous carrier visit may have stemmed from traditional Cape feeling of extra hospitality as the "Tavern of the Seas." The fact that many thousands of Capetonians of all races poured across the visitors' gangway to visit the *Franklin D. Roosevelt*, the entertainment provided at dockside, and the unprecedented donating of blood without regard to race by American crewmen of both races, all contributed to keeping alive friendly ties with individual Americans. But the rebuff the Capetonians *felt* they had received from the American authorities because of domestic political pressure in the United States produced right across provincial lines an anti-U.S. government reaction, which grew in early 1967 despite South African government efforts to play it down.

The current symbol of the decline in provincialism, both in and out of the National Party, was the 1967 election of Eben Dönges as state president. On a purely provincial basis, the Transvaalers would have elected Senator de Klerk. The election of Dönges, long considered a "Cape moderate" and the runner-up to Verwoerd for prime minister, was based upon factors other than party provincial feeling.

Decline of the Right within Afrikanerdom

Although Afrikanerdom is leading the way to unification of all the whites, the movement has been held up from time to time by strong right-wing forces within the *volk*. Dr. Brian du Toit of Stellenbosch University points out that "a change has taken place but that it has not been realised by the *Broederbond* is clear. . . . It is the White man who must regroup to offer a united front against the increasing numbers and growing potential of the African. Instead of changing to a 'White *Broederbond*' which would unite the Whites in this struggle, the *Afrikaner Broederbond* is continuing its fight to assure the position of the Afrikaner and in the process it is causing dissent, suspicion and open hostility within the White population group." [2] Du Toit's criticism of the *Broederbond* and its

[2] From "Politics and Change in South Africa," *International Journal of Comparative Sociology*, March, 1966, published in Dharwar, India.

publication in an India-based journal are an indication that the right wing is under fire from inside Afrikanerdom by people who are not afraid.

Ever since Smuts's wartime victory in 1943, leadership within white politics has come from the right of the political spectrum. The dominant press in South Africa (that in English) has given the lead to the world press in viewing with alarm each new prime minister. After Smuts's internationalism at San Francisco in connection with the creation of the United Nations, Malan appeared to be a narrow isolationist. Yet how almost benign Malan seemed when, following his death, he was succeeded by the "Lion of the North," Strijdom. Press fears of the unintellectual Strijdom were topped by apprehension at the selection of Verwoerd as the cold, calculating leader. But hardly had the assassin's silver knife struck its mortal blow than Dr. Verwoerd took on an almost avuncular character compared to his successor. A Johannesburg rabbi hailed Verwoerd as "one of the greatest prime ministers, if not the greatest South Africa had ever had," while the chief rabbi of Cape Town praised him for providing the "moral basis" of apartheid. Apprehensions concerning Verwoerd's successor were fully equal to those which greeted the earlier Nationalist prime ministers, and there were many who would say that every fear has been justified by events.

Anti-Semitism. However, there are some grave warnings which have yet to be justified. One of these is anti-Semitism. It is significant that State President Dönges, in 1936, strongly opposed the landing of Jewish refugees from Nazi Germany. On the basis of this parallel, historian Keppel-Jones predicted in 1948 that a pogrom would occur in 1956. In fact it was in 1956 that Dönges accepted an invitation to lay the cornerstone of the synagogue in which an overflow crowd mourned the death of Verwoerd in 1966. With the election of the incumbent Prime Minister, many in South Africa and abroad anticipated a new parallel with Nazi Germany. However, when Gus Saron, the general secretary of the Jewish Board of Deputies, was asked in late 1966 by leading Jewish groups in the United States why he felt few Jews would want assistance in fleeing South Africa, he shocked them by comparing Prime Minister

Vorster's wartime anti-British activities with those of the Stern Gang in Palestine.

A case could be made for anti-Semitism in South African white politics in recent years. M.P.'s of Jewish background all sit on the opposition benches with one exception, and include the ablest of debaters. In the 1966 Parliament there were a few ugly remarks by Nationalist backbenchers arising out of the heat of debate. National Party leadership exercised a restraining influence and the Afrikaans press played down the exchanges in reports to their readers.

More serious in awakening haunting memories were the activities during 1967 of a few young Germans—mostly recent immigrants— in Johannesburg. According to newspaper reports the young Germans paid homage to Adolf Hitler. The strong reaction of the Jewish community, including young Jews who marched to a beer hall to give battle, showed that the community would not tolerate neo-Nazism and felt free to speak out and to act.

Prime Minister Vorster gained wide approbation by denouncing anti-Semitic acts and calling upon South Africans not to import the quarrels of Europe into their country (a statement supported by the Jewish Board of Deputies). He acted swiftly through the police to control the incidents and, if possible, to avoid them. Vorster made it explicitly clear that the police would move immediately against anyone—Afrikaners included—who participated in such trouble making. It is probably fair to say that, in its reaction to the Johannesburg incidents, the government's opposition to overt anti-Semitism became more positive than it would have appeared if the incidents had not occurred.

Even more potent in cementing Jewish-Afrikaner relations was the outpouring of support for Israel in the June, 1967, fighting with the Arabs. Jew and Afrikaner united in criticism of Nasser, U Thant, the U.N., Soviet arms, etc. Concrete evidence of support was the South African government's decision to allow the transfer of $8,400,000 of scarce foreign exchange to Israel for humanitarian and charitable purposes at the rate of $1,400,000 per year. The large sum was mostly contributed by South Africa's 100,000-strong Jewry and appears to have far exceeded the per capita support received from Jews of any other nation in support of Israel. The precise breakdown is not known but there were numerous and substantial

Afrikaner gifts for the Israeli cause. Mayors of several overwhelmingly Afrikaner rural towns led fund drives and Dutch Reformed
clergy spoke up for the cause.

It is probably true that at his death Dr. Verwoerd was the most
radical man in his cabinet and, in certain respects, one of the farthest to the left within the spectrum. Mr. Vorster, meanwhile, was
considered to be one of the farthest to the right of the spectrum, an
image reinforced by his role as minister of justice with the police
under his responsibility. So once again the political torch of succession went from the left to the right.

Miners and Farmers. On the right, there are the discontented
groups, such as the miners, who believe that the party has strayed
from its righteous path. Some miners are in revolt against the government's favorable reaction to what amounts to African advance
in the gold mining industry. In 1965–66, these miners scored a few
small victories. However, the "advance" of African miners to positions of greater responsibility and higher pay was resumed in 1967
over the objections of the rebellious miners.

There is right-wing opposition among farmers. Successive ministers of agriculture have been less than popular. Despite the dissatis-
faction which exists in a number of rural constituencies, attempts to
challenge the party by putting up independent or "Republican"
candidates have been futile. The new generation of *Boere* (farmers) have graduated from college, they have inherited the wealth
made by their fathers, and they have seen far more of Europe than
the average American farmer.

Some Afrikaners feel intensely that their great danger comes
from the English. In a 1967 article in *Onderwysblad,* a teaching
journal for the Transvaal and Natal, the director of the prestigious
Suid Afrikaanse Akademie vir Wetenskap en Kuns, concerned with
Afrikaner cultural life and art, charged that over 200,000 Afrikaners
had been anglicized, that Afrikaners remain impoverished "hewers
of wood and bearers of water in our own fatherland," and that
widely read English publications are dangerous carriers of "liberalistic" thoughts.

Churches. It is within the Afrikaans churches that the right has
been most successful. A great tide of ecumenical and liberal

thought emerged at the "Cottesloe" meeting in Johannesburg in 1960, which involved the World Council of Churches. However, not long afterward a strong reaction set in, culminating in a marked retreat into isolationism. Rev. Beyers Naude went from being the honored moderator of the Nederduits Gereformeerde Church in the Transvaal to being defrocked for his views and not even allowed to sit on a school board. The widely publicized (in South Africa) $66,000 libel action against Professor Pont of the University of Pretoria was yet another public airing of the frictions among the clergy and Afrikaans laymen, which date back to the Cottesloe meeting.

Many Afrikaners find it difficult to understand why the major American denominations fail to support enthusiastically the anti-Communist crusade sparked by the Prime Minister's brother, J. D. Vorster, actuary of the Cape Nederduits Gereformeerde Synod. This anti-Communist crusade has been the subject of strong criticism in the Afrikaans press, not for its ideological position, but for its methods and for its divisive nature. A procession of right-wing American churchmen has visited South Africa to speak on Communism, and one of the most popular maintains that the greatest threat to the United States is not Communism but Catholicism. The Afrikaner Calvinist background has created an extremely hostile attitude toward Catholicism. Lectures on the "Dangers of Popery" were given at Stellenbosch University a decade ago. Now, however, the most important consideration in assessing the relative weight of this "Know-Nothing" tradition may prove to be that in 1966–67 Catholic Portugal represented the chief European source of immigrants for South Africa. A decade earlier there were sharp and effective protests against Italian migrants on religious grounds; today the Portuguese, with minimum skills and not too dark complexioned, are welcomed with open arms by the government.

However, the sniping against the immigration policy has built up. The following may be noted from many newspaper comments: "The selection of Greek and Portuguese immigrants must be radically changed. We have no further need for assistants in greengrocer shops." [3] *Die Vaderland* (January 11, 1967) registered a

[3] *Die Transvaler*, January 7, 1967.

complaint that the Minister of Education is "apparently doing nothing to avoid the alarming consequences which the importation of certain immigrants will have in our country." A letter to *Die Beeld* (January 15, 1967) complained of a "hopelessly one sided immigration stream which benefits the English-speaking section of the population only and puts the Afrikaner right back to where he had started." It is a minority view and largely concentrated in the right wing of the Transvaal National Party. Given an economic slump the complaints certainly would grow, but the rate of immigration would also probably decline.

Currently relations in South Africa among the established Christian religions and denominations are friendlier than ever before. The polemics of Father Huddleston (now a bishop in Tanzania), who subsequently reflected that he might have been more effective if less condemnatory, and those of Joost de Blank, now archbishop of Hong Kong, have given way to much more harmonious relations between the Anglicans and the Afrikaans churches. Archbishop de Blank's charge that the Dutch Reformed churches practiced a twisted theology was the cause of much bitterness. It is not within the province of this paper to illustrate the rifts inside the Anglican Church on racial issues—particularly of African versus white communicants—or of the spread and strength of syncretistic movements among Africans. The established churches with their European ties enjoy greater harmony among themselves and are contributing toward drawing the whites closer together. This is said in recognition of post-Cottesloe struggles inside the Afrikaans churches, the public harangue between pro- and anti-apartheid priests and bishops within the Catholic Church, and the strong opposition to separate development expressed by Lutheran pastors (one fourth of whom are white) in their 1967 memorandum. While the changing attitudes of whites are, on the one hand, drawing "their" churches together, they are, on the other hand, creating deeper tensions within the individual churches.

Press. The unification of the whites as a theme must consider also the dialogue between Afrikaner Nationalists and their opponents where agreement does not exist but talk has begun. In this regard the daily exchange of leaders (editorials) in the pro-Nationalist *Die Burger* and the relatively liberal *Cape Times* over the past six years is significant. At times tempers have flared and there has been name-calling in editorials. But the exchange has given the United Party and the Progressives a way to put their ideas before *Die Burger's* Afrikaans-speaking subscribers. Likewise, it has provided the Nationalists with an opportunity to express views (translated into English), even across the most anti-Nationalist breakfast tables, to people who not only dislike Afrikaners but know nothing of their language. It is difficult to ascertain the results of this long exchange. However, a further consequence noted by this observer appears to be the increased thought and caution used in expressing extremely hostile views—knowing the other side would read them. It is open to judgment whether this constitutes better dialogue or even a blunted dialogue in place of no dialogue. Yet it does appear to have contributed to far less Afrikaner vs. English bitterness in the Western Cape Province. A similar approach often has been suggested for Johannesburg but the idea has not taken root.

The proliferation of the right-wing section of the Afrikaans press does not compare with the proliferation of far right publications in the United States, as described in Professor McKay's chapter. When the *South African Observer* (no connection with its London namesake) was first published by S. E. D. Brown, the National Party, hungry for favorable "English"-medium support, provided it with a small subsidy and saw to it that the weekly had favorable displays at railway stations. However, its general line of anti-Semitism and similarity with the John Birch Society and the far right church groups increasingly placed it out of favor with an Afrikaner elite moving toward the political center and greater respectability. The subsidy has long since been dropped, and in 1966 the magazine came under direct counter fire from Afrikaans groups for being a disruptive influence.

The Afrikaans press has on the whole supported white unification with considerable vigor despite the caviling at immigration. *Die Burger*, so often at odds with Dr. Verwoerd, became in 1967 almost the strongest supporter of Mr. Vorster. It has continued to move in a liberal direction (an expression it detests) to the point where it refers to local Africans as "Mr." This elementary courtesy was avoided for the first fifty-five years of South African nationhood, just as it often was in referring to Negroes for a century after the Emancipation Proclamation in the American South.

The English-language press in South Africa continues to hold most of the leadership within the Republic. It is basically conservative but in opposition to the government. Its championing of African aspirations and its chastisement of the government for "petty apartheid" is balanced by a rejection of violence by Africans and their supporters. The unification of the whites has been encouraged by the English press in so far as some papers, such as the *Star*, have displayed some warmth toward the Transkei experiment. The *Rand Daily Mail* and other papers with a more Progressive orientation continue their blanket opposition to the government's domestic policies.

But in foreign affairs the white-controlled press is solidly behind the government in rejecting many attacks at the United Nations and from African nations.

It is reasonable to conclude—despite exceptions to the contrary among miners, farmers, and Dutch Reformed clergy subject to local church control—that the right wing of Afrikanerdom increasingly became disenchanted by the trends which it saw emerging in white politics during the last years of Verwoerd's rule and is so far similarly displeased by their persistence and growth under Mr. Vorster. By comparison with the efforts of "liberal" Afrikaners who have their own criticisms of the National Party, such as its "Coloured Policy," the right-wing element has been unsuccessful in making its displeasure politically effective. It also rails against the youth and lack of parental, church, and university "control." Among the veteran leaders of the most conservative element in Afrikanerdom is the Prime Minister's brother, Dominie Vorster.

The religious minister Vorster has been active in organizing crusades against Communism and opposing "liberalistic" tendencies within Afrikanerdom. The author's conversations with Dominie Vorster, when working on a study of the Dutch Reformed churches, provide some basis for the speculation that, if certain of the recent developments had occurred under Dr. Verwoerd, there would have been strong protests from within the establishment. Yet no such protests have been directed against Prime Minister Vorster. Mutual understanding between the two highly placed brothers may have mollified criticism.

It again must be noted that such trends within Afrikaner or white South African politics pass unnoticed or are felt to be inconsequential by individual Africans and African nations, as well as by most of the world.

New Voices. If the Afrikaner right is at least momentarily in eclipse, it is appropriate to follow this conclusion with some sense of the new voices. The new wind which is affecting elements of white South Africa is not yet a gale. It may dissipate or be quenched. Through the fresh and breezy candor of a staunch Nationalist Afrikaner speaking to the writer we may catch the mood of mid-1967. The individual concerned, who is outside the government and who was active in the violently anti-British Ossewa Brandwag's "storm troopers" during World War II, described the spirit of buoyancy prevalent in some National Party circles in the following way:

John Vorster makes me feel good. He is open-minded, easy, sensible, practical, and reasonable. One realises now what an intellectual dictatorship Verwoerd really ran. Among thinking Afrikaners there is a great sigh of relief now that the new man has come in. Everybody can get moving again: Vorster is tolerant and does not try to run everything, including people's minds. With all this forward-lookingness, however, our right wing has started to rumble—the Albert Hertzogs, Jaap Marais, and all those political nits, even Piet Meyer of S.A.U.K. [Radio South Africa]; who said that Vorster's liberalization of South Africa's international sport policies would lead to "integration" here at home. The "thin edge of the wedge" and all that jazz.

I don't think the right wing will make a go of it. They don't have many ideas, nor much standing, and the feeling of Afrikaner unity above all else is still very strong. Vorster is willing to have a showdown with them and all their sniping; in fact, recently at Bloemfontein he nearly blasted them. At the same time Vorster wants to move strongly on the urban Bantu, get Urban Bantu Councils moving and so on.

The Cape is influencing Vorster very much, and this is all to the good [the speaker is not from the Cape]. The government is wanting to break through to allow white capital into the Bantu areas—if only it can find the proper formula. It also feels a bit uncomfortable about white capital going into Lesotho and Botswana while it cannot go into the Transkei. It is all a time of great hope.

One may ask, By what change of heart does a man of the Afrikaner right move thus to the left? The answer is that there is a high proportion of Ossewa Brandwags and men once of the far right who now stand in the vanguard of new Afrikaner thinking. They are people who always have been more concerned than their less committed friends. It is not inconsistent for an Afrikaner with an anti-British orientation in the 1940s to embrace English-speaking whites in the 1960s and today to share a deep concern for rapprochement with Coloured and then African groups. A sense of political commitment runs through the lives of such men, whose orientation has shifted from pro-Afrikaner to pro-South African.

While this chapter is a summation and analysis of recent white politics, without voluminous supporting documentation, two additional quotations might serve to summarize the content of many others which bear testimony to the central thesis. One comes from a distinguished, highly placed, and respected Afrikaner within the government, a man very much an inside member of the Afrikaner establishment. In mid-1967, in a letter to the writer commenting on developments that have been noted, he wrote:

We are pleased as punch with John Vorster. He is opening up windows to the world quite fearlessly. His right wing is grumbling but is powerless. The about-turn in sport could be seen coming for some time, but it still caught them unawares. They just would not believe such a thing was possible. They are trying to make out now that it is not a change at all. The English press is building John up for all they are worth and that can of course be most embarrassing.

The second quotation is one of many which could be taken from the pro-government Afrikaans press:

The last few years have made us increasingly conscious of the fact that we are not an outpost of Europe, we are not only in Africa but also of Africa. And this knowledge will yet bring about considerable adjustment in our thinking and in our action. We must accept the fact that, before many years have passed, black Africa will be represented by black ambassadors in Cape Town and Pretoria.[4]

The purpose of this essay is not to predict who will win the current argument between the *verligtes* and the *verkramptes* (the enlightened and the narrow-minded) which is sweeping through politics and business, from church to Bantustans, to education and sport and beyond. Our objective, rather, is to emphasize that a critical fact in contemporary white South Africa is the very existence of such a debate over a wide range of crucial issues.

Younger White Voices

Recently, the editor of the *South African Observer* incurred sharp criticism at Stellenbosch University for his bitter attacks on such distinguished Afrikaners as Anton Rupert. Rupert, who resides in and manages his world-wide tobacco empire from this small university town, has helped to restore its eighteenth-century *braak* (square) by repairing charming old Dutch buildings. In supporting Rupert and others under attack, the student body was conserving the traditional Afrikaner right to indulge in a dialogue. This differs from the "liberalism" of certain small groups of students in the last decade, including one led by a cabinet minister's son. What one is observing at the student level is less of a pioneering move and more of a shift in political thinking away from the right toward the center

The yeasty element in Afrikaner college students also comes out in their efforts to escape from the polarization of South African students. The Afrikaanse Studentebond (A.S.B.) has dominated Afrikaans campuses just as the National Union of South African Students (NUSAS) has dominated the English-language campuses. NUSAS has students of all races as members and in its past has been a target of government criticism. Until recently, the farther NUSAS moved to the left—and this included the dynamiting of electrical power pylons by national officers—the farther right the Afrikaans students moved. In 1966–67 the support of young Afri-

[4] *Die Beeld* (Johannesburg), February 2, 1967.

kaners for an accommodation has been met, in part, by NUSAS itself. The president for that period, Margaret Marshall, is a strong
liberal. However, unlike the results of previous years, her winning
platform did not place her to the extreme left of those running for
office. In 1967 the A.S.B. was willing to discuss and debate with
NUSAS, and also to meet with student leaders from African, Coloured, and Indian institutions on a federal basis. The "English"
students constitute a bridge between Afrikaner and African; in time
the Afrikaner and Coloured will create their own bridge.

Prime Minister Vorster has not acted against a bubbling of ideas
among students at Afrikaans institutions as did Dr. Verwoerd.
Those close to Vorster emphasize his sensitivity to youthful opinion
and cite, as an indication of this, the Prime Minister's deep concern
with South Africa's exclusion from some forms of international
sport.

The feelings which animate young people in much of the Western world are having a delayed impact upon South Africa. When
NUSAS invited Senator Robert Kennedy to visit South Africa, it
was the judgment of observers with both liberal and conservative
leanings that rarely had a visitor so captivated the interest of university students. The vice-chancellor of Natal University commented that he had never experienced such intense feelings on the
part of large numbers of students. At Stellenbosch, interest also ran
extremely high, although it would be quite wrong to suggest that
more than a small minority of students agreed with all of Senator
Kennedy's views.

Afrikaans society has been highly traditional, leadership often pa-
triarchal. "Oom Paul" Kruger is a stolid symbol. It has been rare for
youth to be given much of an opportunity in Afrikanerdom. For by
"young man" many Afrikaners mean someone under *forty*. Males in
their teens and twenties have a much lower status in Afrikaner society than in American society. It is this pattern which, rightly or
wrongly, is changing. One study after another, published by market
researchers, sociologists, and in magazine cover stories, tells of a
new dynamism among young white South Africans.

Educational institutions are beginning to play a valuable role in
the formation of new leadership. For the rising politician a univer-

sity education has become more necessary than ever before. It is recognized that it is no longer sufficient for a farmer to enter Parliament untutored in elementary economics. The gradual shift toward placing South Africa's youth into positions of responsibility, the growing prevalence and importance of university education, and the greater mixing of the white youth—all are now indicative of the major role which the universities have assumed in molding the character of the Republic's leadership.

On the "English" liberal side education has always been important. However, this side, defeated at the polls and weakened when a faction resorted to violence, is not the only channel through which universities can develop the concepts of leadership. It is bilingualism which, in addition to promoting white unity, represents an influential force in shaping a leadership that is less parochial, more tolerant, and more concerned with the country as a whole.

The sharp increase which has occurred in the percentage of students who speak English at home but attend Afrikaans universities, and the numbers of Afrikaans-speaking students who attend English-medium institutions, is yet another factor promoting white unity. Many parents deliberately encourage their sons and daughters to attend college in the opposite medium. In other cases, such as English-speaking forestry students at Stellenbosch, the changeover is because the course of study is not available in their home language.[5]

The younger white voices naturally make themselves heard through many professional channels and not always in one youthful chorus. It is the younger Afrikaner writers (*Die Sestigers*—Men of the Sixties) who have grown in power through their constructive criticism of South African society. The rise of the contemporary Afrikaans novel, as a political force equal to the Afrikaans poetry of the late nineteenth and early twentieth centuries, is more easily understood in countries with a stronger political-literary tradition than

[5] The pattern in African education is quite different—for example, the emphasis there is upon ethnic separation into Xhosa, Zulu, Sotho, etc.—and still continues to move away from the older South African pattern at Cape Town and Witwatersrand of academically integrated education. The impact of the ethnic institutions upon African leadership is quite different, but that is not part of this paper.

that of the United States. Within Afrikanerdom, writers constitute
the opposition in a manner which bears a closer parallel to the role
of writers in the Soviet Union than is true of Great Britain or the
United States.

Afrikaner and Coloured poets publish in the same Afrikaans
journals and together in anthologies. They also have some personal
contacts. Greater freedom exists for young painters and sculptors in
Cape Town, Johannesburg, and Durban who mingle at each other's
exhibits, collect, admire, and attack works of art regardless of race.
South Africa's population is becoming statistically younger. Of long-
range consequence is the rise of younger voices accompanying a si-
lent shift downwards in decision making. The white voices do seem
free of much of the emotionalism of the past and prepared to seek
new solutions to old problems.

Changes in Afrikaner Goals and the Widening Laager

In addition to the forces which we have discussed, a change in
Afrikaner goals has further stimulated the unification of the white
oligarchy. This, perhaps, is not so much a change as a realization
that virtually all the original goals have been achieved. The language fight was fierce until Afrikaans was made official in 1925; an
equal South African flag was attained in 1928; the Union Jack dis-
appeared in 1958; and a Republic was born on May 31, 1961. Another development which reflects this new attitude is the lessened
influence of the *Broederbond* (including a discontinuance of national meetings) as the continued dominance of the National Party
undercuts the original need for a shadow cabinet. The F.A.K.
(Federasie van Afrikaanse Kultuurvereniginge) is concerned almost as much with fostering good relations with English-speaking
whites as with its traditional task of perpetuating Afrikaans culture.
One of the few unrealized goals, and one not shared by all Nationalists, is the extension of "Christian National Education," a prin-
cipal source of current disagreement among Afrikaners and, particularly, between the National Party and the United Party, which so
long opposed it.

After 1961, although Afrikanerdom continued to look for greater

success in business and in a few other areas, by and large the traditional goals had been transmuted into broader South African goals.
The United Party had been steam-rollered in one session of Parliament after another. Rightly or wrongly, the old animosities were
dead issues. Once thoroughly beaten by an adversary, the loser
sometimes is more willing to shake hands and get along than might
be the case if he had another round to the contest. The Nationalist
drive has lost its original head of steam. The United Party has been
able to remain in opposition, so its passion of 1953—"Vote for the
right to vote again"—has waned. Together in many respects—
although one does not notice this in the gallery of Parliament—the
two parties lead the white electorate. Progressive Party supporters,
unwilling to acquiesce, have been forced to accept the altered circumstances or to cease to exist as a party. The South African antigovernment press has moved a long way toward accepting many
ideas to which, at first, it was opposed. This change applies to the
attitude of the English-language press toward the Republic, to laws
against sabotage, to some forms of detention without trial, in varying degrees to the concept of Bantustans, and, particularly, to a
modification of its opposition to South Africa's defense budget,
which has grown rapidly from an insignificant figure to one whose
percentage is approaching that of the Soviet Union, the United
States, Egypt, or Israel.

Today, the attitude of the English press in South Africa toward
Prime Minister Vorster is quite different from the attitude which is
conveyed by the press of most Western nations—a difference more
marked than was ever true of Dr. Verwoerd prior to his death.
Usually the Western press portrays Vorster as a hard, cruel-lipped,
Bible-pounding man with a Nazi past whose first name is Balthazar. In contrast, the English press in South Africa leans toward
an image of an efficient politician: effective in stopping sabotage
and controlling crime; a man who enjoys his weekly round of golf
and from whose lips come humorous observations on his own and
other humans' foibles. The difference is summed up in the way the
New York *Times* generally refers to him as Balthazar J. Vorster,
and the Johannesburg Sunday *Times* as John Vorster or B. J. Vorster.

The fulfillment of the old Afrikaner goals has meant that the chief goal today simply is the retainment of what has been achieved. It is perhaps logical, and often has been predicted, that this would lead South Africans into what one recent study has been titled: *The White Laager*. The laager mentality is that of isolation, of remaining within the circle of ox wagons while the Indians (Africans, the whole world) encircle them and shoot arrows (spears, rockets). There is an element in Afrikanerdom which looks toward a future in which it heroically goes down in flames, fighting to the last breath.

But there is not a *Götterdämmerung* mood about white politics in the Republic today. It is much more a reaching out, a movement toward a larger laager. At the closing of Parliament two years ago, Dr. Dönges caught the spirit of this movement when he spoke of five million hearts beating as one. Simple arithmetic shows that his laager, if laager it was, included all the whites plus the Coloured and Indian populations. Of course, it is open to debate whether this movement will succeed or even be sustained. Yet it has been an underlying mood for almost three years, years during which precious little has been done to implement implied promises to the smaller minority groups. The white political thrust has not concerned itself primarily with the non-white minorities, although it may be turning in that direction.

If the whites really are trying to enlarge the laager, their approach to Coloured and Indians will be intensified. The government will place even greater emphasis upon the dangers to the minority communities existing in what the whites will argue may be a theoretically nonracial society but which, in practice, would be African dominated. In their effort to achieve a nonracial society or power for themselves, many African leaders have resorted to threats against the non-white minorities, which has produced among some individuals a fear of African rule and a subsequent identification with the whites. The withdrawal of the colonial power (to assume for the moment Leo Marquard's thesis of white South Africa as a colonial power within its own borders) has not always created a salubrious climate for the minorities. One does hear among Indians concern about the fate of Arabs in Zanzibar, however much deserved, and of Indians in Tanzania. Fears of African rule are sometimes no less rampant among Coloureds than among whites, and are fed by the same kind of stereotypes and interpretations of events as used in the rest of Africa. Whites exploit the Coloured fear of physically stronger Africans in competition for jobs in which Coloureds are now protected. As a result of the government's laws on influx control, a serious imbalance has occurred in the cities, with males greatly outnumbering females. Among the Africans in the main centers of Coloured population, this has led to sex competition between Coloured and African men. More than one Coloured leader has characterized his people as standing between the devil and the deep blue sea.

The tremendous improvement in Coloured living standards since the 1950s (when poor whites pushed poor Coloureds out of menial jobs) has done more to "prepare" the Cape Coloured community for entry into the larger non-African grouping rather than succeeding in actually moving them into it.

The concept of Group Areas has been a particular cause of irritation to the Coloured community of Cape Town. Another has been their gradual exclusion from various courses of study at Cape Town University. In their bitterness, the Coloured leaders had the support of many Cape whites including Cape Afrikaners. The rift between the white government and the Coloured community only now is being alleviated gradually through the improvements in education, housing, employment, and other nonpolitical spheres. The unification of the whites and their broader acceptance of separate development has not been without its impact upon the "brown Afrikaners." Most dramatic of the individual changes is that of Dr. Richard van der Ross. Long a thorn in the government's side, Dr. van der Ross was the most articulate Coloured proponent of the Progressive Party's goals. His 1967 decision to join the government, as the best way to forward the aspirations of his people, naturally was hailed by *Die Burger* and *Die Beeld* as a triumph for (1) the policy of separate development and (2) the need to bring the Coloured community into harmony with the Afrikaner.

A projection of the new outlook within Afrikanerdom was given by David P. de Villiers, leader of the successful South African legal team at The Hague, in a speech in Pretoria on April 26, 1967. Although many of the ideas expressed had been circulating previously in the Cape, it was a significant move for such a speech, based upon "dynamic change" and "flexibility," to be given to the Afrikaner establishment in Pretoria. The invitation which Piet Cillie, editor of Cape Town's *Die Burger,* received a month before to make a speech of a similar nature at the highly conservative Potchefstroom University in western Transvaal reflected another important change in current attitudes. A year earlier neither man would have been invited to give a speech which could possibly suggest such a degree of change.

Advocate de Villiers' speech (in Afrikaans) said *inter alia:*

For a long time it was necessary to make a laager and to insist on the principle of noninterference in domestic [household] matters. Such a policy has many advantages . . . it showed we were determined . . we had time to build physical defences . . . we could build and adopt policies. It also had disadvantages such as creating the impression that we didn't have answers to some attacks on our policy. The laager idea could never be permanent . . . a completely inward looking person can never live fully . . . this is also true of a nation and especially in modern circumstances. One needs healthy communications with the world not only for economic reasons but because of the spirit of man. It was difficult to decide when to give up the laager but the South West Africa case began an opening out process. We learned that we could practice this with success. But opening up takes a lot more manpower than you need when you are closed in. It is a gigantic task to answer accusations and misrepresentations in U.N. reports, various seminars . . . International Labour organization . . . Committee of Jurists, etc. It requires the involvement of many people outside the government among makers of public opinion. Our policy is not static but developing. We must acknowledge imperfections . . . that some situations are less than ideal. But we can change and grow from the inside . . . be able to tolerate internal differences of viewpoint as policies adjust . . . so that we can contribute constructively to living together in southern Africa.

When questioned by the writer, Advocate de Villiers said with conviction, "We do listen to persuasion. We are debating among ourselves. Allow us to debate without forcing us." Without doubting the sincerity of this distinguished Afrikaner, an observer must note that white South Africans have been pleading for "time" for almost fifty years. Hitherto "time" has not resulted in major steps toward solving the problem. The current internal debate within the Afrikaner section is, admittedly, the freest and most pregnant with change of any since the National Party came into power in 1948. Nevertheless, however optimistic an observer of white politics is about the chance for peaceful evolution, he must voice the skeptic's "show me."

In order to create a broadening laager, whites may extend the "fear" stratagem, so successful in unifying their own ranks, to the Indians, to the Coloureds, and to some of the smaller and weaker African tribes. This is one of the arguments used by the whites to encourage Bantustans. The discrimination already practiced by Swazis against their Zulu cousins in the police, education, and other civil service posts has resulted in Zulus receiving the "golden hand-shake" along with the whites. Thus, given the vested interests of tribes in Bantustans and, particularly, the African establishment in power within a Bantustan, the whites may well be successful in their strategy. In the past they have played the traditional chiefs off against African nationalists. However, it is a significant refinement to play this blend of tribal-regional-modern African leader off against the unitary African leadership, much of it in prison or exile.

If one peers into the future, the broadening of the laager may be followed with an opening up, as it was in the Boers' famous 1838 battle against the Zulu Chief, Dingaan, when the horsemen rode out of the laager, as defense shifted to offense. In this century, the offensive into Africa would be one of friendship and trade in an effort to win acceptance. At the moment there are no indications of any territorial ambitions and many disavowals of them. Although from 1910 to the 1960s, South Africa coveted the former High Commission Territories, Dr. Verwoerd succeeded in allaying most fears with a categorical renunciation of this earlier goal.

Thus the unification of the white oligarchy appears now to be the prelude to an attempted enlargement of that oligarchy. Whether this is indeed a goal and whether beyond it lies a viable political system which will allow Africans political fulfillment, the white government has felt a compelling need for a New Foreign Policy to match the realities of New White Politics.

NEW FOREIGN POLICY

White unification, so obviously accelerated by threats of foreign intervention, is also a precondition for a "white" foreign policy. At this stage, it is difficult to foresee how far beyond the confines of South Africa any domestic widening of the laager along the lines discussed will, in fact, extend. South Africa remains the graveyard for the prophecies of the social scientists. Historian C. W. de Kiewiet, dean of South African observers, postulated in 1965 that "apartheid is a pessimistic creed. It is defensive, not aggressive. Under pressure it is more likely to retreat than attack. Its movement is in the direction of its own mental laager." [6] In so saying Dr. de Kiewiet correctly described the attitude which prevailed a few years ago. However, during the intervening time there have been significant explorations beyond the laager. They are dependent upon the solid domestic "white base." Whether they will be extended or fade away only time will tell.

The Foundation for Dynamic Change

A "white," i.e., not a purely National Party, policy has existed with respect to the relationship of South West Africa to the world. In this sphere, Sir De Villiers Graaff, leader of the United Party, has cooperated with and been kept informed by the government. The major white parties have recognized South West Africa as political dynamite and excluded it from inflammatory party debate. But beyond this, further cooperation has not been forthcoming. Membership in the Commonwealth of Nations proved to be a divisive force within the white oligarchy. The contention that until there was agreement at home disagreement abroad would be catastrophic seems to have been proved by events.

United Party distrust of Nationalist foreign operations has been especially conspicuous in annual debates on the Information Service budget vote. Only in recent years has a majority of United Party members accepted the idea of such a service in peacetime.

[6] Cornelis W. de Kiewiet, "South Africa's Gamble," *Virginia Quarterly Review* (Winter, 1965), p. 9.

The growth of the South African foreign service has been described elsewhere.[7] In the period between the independent Boer Republics and 1927, the country had no foreign representation. Gradually, following this, a corps of men capable of implementing a foreign policy began to emerge. In 1937–38, one of them, Charles te Water, was chairman of the League of Nations Assembly. Suffice it to say that in recent years the South African foreign service has been markedly strengthened and now is about 10 percent the size of the U.S. foreign service.

While the foreign service may have the technical knowledge, a new foreign policy requires backing in the nonofficial sphere. Afrikaners have created various organizations to meet their changing needs. The *Broederbond,* organized in 1918, was designed as a kind of shadow government to counteract the English domination of the official sphere. The *Reddingsdaadbond* emerged in the 1930s to tackle the problem of the poor white Afrikaner. SABRA (in English it stands for the South African Bureau of Racial Affairs) had its origin in Stellenbosch in 1947, with F.A.K., which had already started thinking of the need to study racial problems, contributing the first £100. For years, SABRA was the fountainhead of ideas on separate development, even when its more advanced thinkers ran ahead of the tempo set by the National Party and control was seized by less radical government supporters, who moved SABRA headquarters to Pretoria.

In the same tradition of evolving an organization to meet a need, the Africa Study Institute in Pretoria was begun when a major impetus was provided through the direction of W. C. Du Plessis, after his ambassadorship in Washington, and before he became administrator of South West Africa. The Institute, operating primarily in the private sector, has endeavored to bring a knowledge of black Africa to leading Afrikaners. Although the Institute's political bulletins on Africa might sometimes strike Americans as naïve and at other times as propagandistic, its maps and atlases represent sound scholarship. Also preparing the seedbed for a new direction in Afrikaner thinking has been the development of African study

---

[7] Edwin S. Munger, *Notes on the Formation of South African Foreign Policy* (Pasadena, The Castle Press, 1965).

courses in Afrikaans universities. If they have yet to match the distinction enjoyed by Africanists in the English-language universities,
their impact on Afrikaner thinking has been significant. Dr. Malan,
when he was prime minister in 1954, like most educated South
Africans, was only vaguely familiar with the location of most West
African countries. Europe yes, Africa no. Stellenbosch University
offered no course of study on Africa. Yet, a decade later Dr.
Malan's widow was studying the latest American textbooks on West
Africa as part of an extensive African Studies Program at Stellenbosch.

This preparation was matched in both the Afrikaans and the
English press. Both stepped up their coverage of African news. The
Johannesburg *Star*'s Africa Service produces some of the best re-
porting on the Congo and Central Africa. *News/Check* magazine
was founded in 1962 with two goals: to make Southafricans
(*News/Check* spelling) conscious of Africa, and to report the
domestic scene without aligning itself with any party. Its capital
was divided deliberately between Afrikaans- and English-speaking
South Africans. Its editor then and now, Otto Krause, studied at
Stellenbosch, Oxford, and Yale, and prepared for his job with a
long tour of tropical Africa. *News/Check*'s circulation in southern
Africa trails that of *Time* but exceeds that of *Newsweek*, and it has
provided many educated South Africans with a significant window
onto African affairs.

Such a background to a new foreign policy is no guarantee of
either its rightness or its success. But the new policy did not spring
full-blown in response to a sudden need. In fact, the new policy
tends to proceed cautiously, stopping at critical moments lest it
make an error either in regard to internal political pressures or to
some incident which would attract lightning from a hostile world.

International Sports

The handling of international sports also has been part of the
white government's preparation for a diplomatic offensive in Africa.
It is both a hot domestic issue and one with far-reaching implications for South African foreign policy. South Africa's exclusion from

the 1964 Tokyo Olympics was a shock to the sports-loving whites. The government, in an effort to find a formula which would mollify its international critics but not alienate its domestic supporters, had agreed to send a partially integrated team—at least people of all races were to be on the same team—for the first time in South African history. In preparation for the Olympics, a party of African trackmen toured Great Britain with success. Also, a Coloured weight lifter appeared certain of inclusion on the team and a possible medal in Tokyo.

However, the government hesitated over such questions as common blazers, the team going as two contingents or one, and the problems of domestic trials. The final rejection of the South African adaptations was basically political. On the one hand, it was argued by some liberals in South Africa and amongst overseas critics that a team of African, white, Indian, and Coloured sportsmen representing "their" country would be beneficial to the cause of racial tolerance. On the other hand, it also would represent an acknowledgment by the world of a South African policy that would have political overtones. The technical rejection put forward by the Olympic Committee was based on a lack of integrated selection procedures—a point which South Africa might now be prepared to adopt. The added criticism that there are universities where sports are not integrated would be unacceptable to the authorities. It is a charge which could be laid—to a far less degree—against the United States and some other countries.

In 1967 South Africa was placed in a position of either more isolation in international sports or of allowing visiting teams, and South African teams going abroad, to choose on the basis of over-all merit instead of merit within a racial group.

The decision to allow the brilliant South African-born Coloured cricketer, "all-rounder" Basil d'Oliveira, to tour with Britain's M.C.C. in South Africa was a step in a liberalizing direction. D'Oliveira, who had been welcomed as a coach for non-whites in South Africa, had protested restrictions on white spectators watching him play with non-white teams. If he had been denied entry as a member of the British team it is likely that the tour would have been canceled.

In rugby, a similar decision of a step up or down had to be taken. The famous New Zealand All Blacks traditionally have used Maori stars when playing against South Africa's Springboks in home matches but not in South Africa. In 1958 the writer asked sports editors in leading New Zealand cities whether or not the time would come when the "All Blacks" could no longer be "all white" in South Africa. Most editors rather accurately estimated a decade, although at that time there was almost no agitation in New Zealand for a change in the pattern of the international matches. South Africa's expressed willingness to accept Maori players at home could have long-range consequences. In the past, many enthusiastic Coloured and some African fans have cheered for the visiting team with a vociferousness that had political overtones, and the question of barring non-white spectators remains a source of potential trouble. Another rugby question involves the Japanese national junior varsity. Behind the scenes the Japanese have been trying to arrange a rugby tour similar to that of the Argentine junior varsity. The South African government has stalled and made excuses. If the government continues to stall, the price it will have to pay in terms of the important and growing commercial ties between South Africa and Japan may be stiff. During 1967, problems in international swimming, golf, and tennis began to yield to a more pragmatic approach toward relaxing racial restrictions. Nevertheless, South Africa constantly is seeking a means of reestablishing international affiliations in football (soccer) without integration. There have been, and are, then, indications that the South African government's change toward new policies in most international sports will persist, but there have been moves of this nature before which have later proved false.

All of South Africa's international representatives can now wear the same uniforms and the "Springbok" or national sporting emblem. This change, together with the establishment of the non-white liaison committees, merely scratches the surface.

The Prime Minister, in announcing new ground rules for international sports, did so in a typically Afrikaner style. He reached back through South African history to cite a few isolated examples in the last forty years when Maoris and other non-whites have

competed in South Africa against whites. The essence of the Afrikaner political style is to pronounce that what one will be doing in
the future (however radically changed) is just about what one always has done. Sophisticated Afrikaners often smile at this trait,
but on the international scene the argument that in fact no change
is involved sometimes is naïvely accepted.

The White Diplomatic Offensive

South Africa's major diplomatic offensive in Africa got off the
ground in 1966–67, although an earlier effort had been made before
the wave of African independence began to gather momentum. In
an attempt to break the ice in 1957, South Africa's Foreign Minister
(waspish but highly professional Eric Louw) lunched with Kwame
Nkrumah. Following this, in 1958, Nkrumah spent some time seriously discussing the merits of sending such a man as his cabinet
chief, Robert Gardiner, as high commissioner to Pretoria.[8] That
idea was stillborn in part because of schooling problems for the
Gardiners' small children. An attempt to provide nondiscriminatory
treatment has led the government to announce plans for diplomatic
suburbs in Pretoria and in Cape Town.

The South African government has every right to be nervous
when a distinguished African leader (such as Seretse Khama, when
his plane had to land unexpectedly in 1963) or an American Negro
begins to move around unaccompanied by someone who can
explain—the irony is obvious—that the dark-skinned man is a for-
eigner. The government solution to this is that accredited African
diplomats come without their families on brief stays, and reside in
top-flight hotels where they can be protected from possible insult.
This is by way of admission that, while the public has been prepared for new steps, little change has in fact taken place in domestic relationships, and hence the danger of an incident remains
great. Even wives of visiting Japanese diplomats have experienced
difficulties of this nature and have been excluded from the country,
much to the embarrassment of those concerned with the expanding
South African–Japanese trade.

[8] The author was present during some of Nkrumah's Accra discussions.

Nevertheless, it is important to note the trend of increasing so-phistication in white South African politics toward black Africa. The white public no longer sorts out "good guys" on the old basis of pigmentation alone. Tshombe was a hero to many of the Afri-kaner youths who served his cause. Questioned by the writer in the recruiting hall about being under African leadership, they rejoined, "Ag, man, hy is 'n gawe kêrel" (a nice guy). While the government cautiously took over a whole floor of the best Bloemfontein hotel for Prime Minister Matanzima's visit so that his entourage need not enter the dining room, many Free Staters, who regard him as a friend of South Africa, said they did not mind where he dined as long as he was not what they call an "agitator type."

To a considerable extent the new, less prejudiced, view of the Bantu peoples derives from political necessity. But it is due at least as much to the favorable—but not fawning—impression which educated Africans, as well as dignified tribal people, are making upon white South Africans. The Transkeian leaders are making a distinct psychological impact upon white public opinion. Whites are genuinely proud of the leading role which "our own Bantu" are playing in world sport, literature, and even within the context of Pan-Africanism. There is an acceptance, so obvious to observers who are more or less free of racial stereotypes, that many Africans have similar desires and value systems to those of the white oligarchy. Afrikaners do recognize that there are value systems within African societies which some Africans prefer to those of white South Africa. One American approach to the red Indian—you are free to be like me but not free to be different—rarely is considered as a measuring stick in approaching the societies of southern Africa. All this being true, the prejudice among the great majority of white South Afri-cans is such that their recognition of a "Bantu way of life" is per-ceived and encouraged not so much out of good will but as a rationalization of the whites' desire to remain separate. Thus, this line of reasoning, which is so characteristic of some Afrikaners, does not carry convincing weight with those who visit South Africa from abroad.

The paternalism so often evident in white South Africa's attitude toward the Transkei—a paternalism of those who support and also of those who oppose Bantustans—is a barrier to the new foreign policy. In spite of this the attitudinal change toward Africans continues. When Prime Minister Vorster's beautiful blonde daughter was married in 1967, her wedding dress was made by the same Afrikaans woman who made the wedding dress of the Transkeian Prime Minister's niece a few months before. Such a linking in common humanity would not have been reported a few years ago. This is just one of the many discrete changes taking place internally which appear to add up to nothing and yet are laying a foundation for changes in white actions.

Southern African Neighbors

Early in the development of the Bantustan or separate development policy, white leadership in the Republic realized that the Transkei example, and subsequent Bantustans, would be open to the charge of South African intimidation, especially since for some years to come three fourths of the budget would have to be supplied by Pretoria if economic development were to take place at all. One by-product of a program of economic help to, and harmonious relations with, the former High Commission Territories could be that, if South African *bona fides* were proven in Lesotho or Botswana, they might be accepted as examples of what a future Transkei or Ovambostan might look like given political independence.

Lesotho, Botswana, Swaziland. The economic leverage which South Africa could exert on the independent states is scarcely less than that which is true of the Bantustans. However, Ghanaian Robert Gardiner, now executive secretary of the U.N. Economic Commission for Africa, said on a 1967 visit to Lesotho that he found no fear of South African interference among the Basuto.

Cooperation with the three territories was held up by Dr. Verwoerd's insistence on strict protocol—independence before talks. Thus, in Lesotho, the Ox Bow scheme to sell clean water and power to South Africa's water-short Witwatersrand was not investigated intensively until 1967, although years before Minister of Defense Jim Fouche and Chief Jonathan had gone on a camping trip together in the area and technical people in South Africa had discussed the concept.

Lesotho's appointment of Afrikaner industrialist Anton Rupert, lawyer Dennis Cowen,[9] and Natal University head Owen Horwood as economic advisers is only one of many unofficial ties developing between white South Africa and Lesotho. Considerable publicity accompanied the historic visit of Lesotho's Prime Minister Jonathan to Cape Town for talks with Prime Minister Vorster and other South African ministers. (South African officials have complained that such newspapers as the New York *Times* did not give much play to the visit. However, at the time of the visit the *Times* could not obtain a visa for a resident correspondent following the expulsion of their man for writing what the South Africans felt were poisonous and biased articles.)

South Africa's direct economic assistance has been limited to sending a substantial gift of corn to Lesotho to alleviate a food shortage, and to sending veterinarians to Swaziland to stamp out foot-and-mouth disease. Although in the latter case it was in South Africa's economic self-interest to control the disease, the spirit of helping is genuine. So far, the new South African interest has not done much materially for Botswana but direct help is expected. Botswana's ambassador to Washington and to the United Nations, Z. K. Mathews, is a South African by birth and extremely knowledgeable about the Republic from long years of involvement in African politics. He finds no problems in visiting South Africa and, rather surprisingly, keeps a colorful South African Information Service calendar on his New York desk. His low-key approach to South Africa—while not condoning apartheid in any form—is based upon his own and his government's assessment of Botswana's self-interest.

The scope of the thrust toward the north generated within South Africa's white oligarchy was illustrated by the chairman of the Progressive Party in an address to the 1967 annual conference of the

[9] It was Professor Cowen, formerly of Cape Town Law School and subsequently on the faculty of the University of Chicago, who, visiting South Africa in 1964, wrote a series of articles for the Johannesburg *Star* giving his changed image of South Africa and expressing "grounds for optimism" concerning white South Africa's capacity for change.

governing Botswana Democratic Party. The Progressive leader said that Botswana "can become the vital bridge between us and the great continent of Africa to which we belong and from which we are so tragically cut." He added that Botswana should enlarge the field of contact between black Africa and South Africa because "the more you boycott and isolate South Africa, the stronger apartheid becomes."

The most likely area for Botswana–South African cooperation lies in water resources. The tripartite talks, including Portugal, which took place in Pretoria on technical problems of the joint utilization of rivers, particularly concerned the Okavango. Now it is possible that major South African financial aid will be forthcoming for the long proposed argicultural development of Botswana's Okavango Swamp.

Malawi and Beyond. The 1967 economic treaty with Malawi involves another financially weak state comparable to Lesotho, but one that certainly was not compelled to send three cabinet ministers to Cape Town to be wined and dined by white cabinet ministers and then to return the hospitality. The preparation of the white South African public, especially the rural Afrikaner section, has succeeded thus far in dampening criticism of unprecedented pictures, beginning with such an elementary one as Dr. Verwoerd shaking hands with Kaiser Mantanzima, and proceeding to *Die Burger's* picture of Prime Minister Vorster and Foreign Minister Muller interspersed among three Malawi ministers. For anyone who is accustomed to a comparatively nonracial society, the significance may be lost. But in white South Africa the impact of such pictures and the actions surrounding them could create a change in public thinking far greater than the often referred to introduction into major league baseball after World War II of Jackie Robinson and other American Negro stars.

The Malawi treaty provided an occasion to define certain South African relationships, as South Africa claims they will evolve, with other African states. In reply to a statement by Malawi Commerce and Industry Minister J. T. Kumbweza, that his country did not want to be a "banana republic," Minister Haak assured the Malawians that South Africa was interested only in encouraging productive development. *Die Burger*'s columnist "Dawie" (March 14, 1967) approved this position and explained to its readers that what Mr. Kumbweza meant was that Malawi would not fall into the kind of relationship with South Africa that the United States has had with some Central American countries.

The parliamentary discussion over the Malawi arrangements also provided Prime Minister Vorster with an opportunity to reiterate that he intends to treat the visiting head of any African state, no matter what its size or the color of its leader's skin, in the same fashion as Prime Minister Jonathan and the Malawi ministers have been received. The arrival of a Malawi ambassador in Pretoria means less, because he is white, than the cordial acceptance of his black deputy. Transition to a black ambassador is expected. The South African Prime Minister endorsed Sir Seretse Khama's statement that when the two men met it would be man to man, not father to son, and as leaders of equally independent states. Mr. Vorster's stated intention of visiting Malawi and other African states which have sent representatives to South Africa would mark another major breakaway from a simple laager policy.

We have noted the great change in attitude toward "outside" Africans during the Nationalist tenure in office. It would be naïve to believe that South Africa is being altruistic. Indeed, Minister Haak has referred to the undesirability of "charity." A distinction *can* be drawn between genuine aid with no strings attached, as Haak puts it, which will help another country but is of enormous political advantage to the helping country, and self-interested aid motivated by a desire to dominate an economy and to provide the donor with economic leverage for political ends.

So far, South Africa's economic treaty with Malawi and the contracts with various South African firms for construction there have been hailed as the high-water mark of the diplomatic offensive. At one time, industrial tycoon Harry Oppenheimer had hopes for contact with Zambia, but despite South Africa surpassing Rhodesia and Britain as the leading exporter to Zambia, the political climate remains mild at best. Many South African efforts farther north in Africa are clothed in secrecy, although there are a number of individual examples of trade relationships. Amongst these the Congo and the Ivory Coast stand out. South African commercial participation in Mauritanian copper is another contact. The resignation of Kenya Vice President Joseph Murumbi, to head Rupert's Rothman's Tobacco operation in the East African country, was a business move that has attracted notable comment.

Rhodesia. Inevitably, white South African politics are inextricably linked with Rhodesian questions. What stands out in the new foreign policy has been the reluctance with which South Africa has officially helped the Ian Smith regime. Dr. Verwoerd strongly cautioned Smith from attempting a Unilateral Declaration of Independence (U.D.I.). South Africa has failed to recognize Rhodesia. In the 1966 election, the United Party was outspoken in calling for South African assistance to Rhodesia. The Nationalists generally had little to say. Dr. Verwoerd wanted no part of the controversial tanker *Johanna V* when it moved from off Mozambique to stand off Durban. The position of the National Party has been that it may be prepared to swim with Rhodesia but not to sink with it. After the 1966 election, *Die Burger* began openly to criticize U.D.I. and to oppose South African involvement. Nationalist cabinet ministers have spoken privately of the lack of a moral basis, as they see it, for the Smith regime's policy toward Africans. Although emotions among the South African white public have run extremely high in support of the Rhodesian Front, the white leaders of South Africa apparently take a different view. In essence they might even prefer to have a sympathetic, and possibly economically dependent, African government in Rhodesia to one where whites ruled by force and became a storm center of world opinion. Certainly there have been no bars on the sale of South African goods to Zambia as a counter to the partial Zambian boycott of Rhodesia. To force the Rhodesians to the point of collapse, at the price of proving that sanctions work in southern Africa, is a price South Africa will not pay in full. But as the unified white oligarchy now views Rhodesia, the continuance of the Rhodesian dispute is a barrier to expanding the new foreign policy.

South West Africa. The marked change in the South African government's attitude toward the problem of South West Africa was stimulated in part by the late Dag Hammarskjold. The whole story might be different today if he had lived. The U.N. Secretary General and Prime Minister Verwoerd expressed deep respect for each other. It was Hammarskjold's fairness, the questions he asked, and the fact that Dr. Verwoerd was not always given acceptable answers by his own administration which caused the South African Premier to take a longer look. He did not like everything he saw and soon launched the massive plan for economic development. The controversial political aspects of the Odendaal Plan do not obscure the economic changes, particularly the buying up of "white" land for African use. The Ovambostan step was to be expected.

These moves were entrusted to Administrator Du Plessis by Dr. Verwoerd as being of crucial importance to South Africa. The immense sigh of relief at the "no-decision success" of the South African team at The Hague reflected, at least in part, the white oligarchy's recognition that its position was threatened. Dr. Verwoerd did take extraordinary steps to muster the best available talent and he did not spare expense in presenting the South African case.

But what of white opinion within South West Africa? In time, this may be of vital importance. In the past the relationship of South Africa to South West Africa has had many colonial overtones. Civil servants spoke of "going home," and they "served" tours of duty. The administrator was more like a "governor" than an administrator of the provinces. Although born Southwesters (used in the local sense of white inhabitants) rarely have held the key positions, for years the legislature has had more indigenous flavor than is true of the provinces. The 1967 controversy between South West Africa and South Africa over the fishing rights of South African factory ships operating in South West African territorial waters stands as part of a long tradition of distinctions in the minds of Southwesters.

The significant German minority has cooperated with the government during good times, but should pressure be placed on South West Africa the Germans cannot be counted on to react precisely

in the manner Afrikaners would react. The Germans have not held
political power for half a century. Their chief concern is a stable
political environment within which there can be economic prosperity. Few of them are really concerned with the goals and aspirations of Afrikanerdom. Yet their apprehension at the prospect, as
they see it, of relatively uneducated Africans assuming the reins of
government or of an imposed U.N. administration, which might be
equally chaotic or at least discriminate against them, is just as
strong as among Afrikaners. The Germans responded favorably to
the extra representation which Dr. Malan arranged for South West
African whites in the Union (now Republican) parliament, as well
as to the customs advantages extended. Furthermore, Du Plessis
has been the best administrator South West Africa has known after
several less than top-class men.

The really tiny "English" minority is itself split into various
English-speaking nationalities. Windhoek is a cosmopolitan city,
especially compared to cities of comparable size in the Republic.
There is a mixture of Afrikaners, Germans (not as aristocratic as
was true when Germany ruled and South West Africa was the
upper-class colony compared to Togo or German East Africa), and
English (including a small but important subgroup of people of
Jewish origin from Eastern Europe), who mix more freely with one
another than is true in the Republic proper. On the other hand,
there is less contact with the non-white community than in, say,
Johannesburg or Cape Town. Educated Hereros, Ovambos, Da-
maras, etc., usually leave South West Africa for one reason or another, and there are few intellectual equals to match the white
establishment.

In recent years, the white community of South West Africa has
grown closer together than ever before. While there is little talk of
separation from South Africa, there is continuing criticism of the
distant "Praetorian guard" in the handling of local grievances.
Against this, the white element has been welded closer together by
a number of factors, including the current affluency (partly a reflection of U.N. pressure and subsequent South African government
spending), and a common rejection of the occasionally rather
bloodthirsty speeches made against South West Africa by some

African leaders and their white allies. As far as achieving a possible dialogue is concerned, it is unfortunate that statements about South West Africa are filtered by the press (perhaps not for ulterior purposes but because of shock news value) so that reasoned comments do not come through. Broadcasts of South West African exiles on Peking Radio are given fuller play than a thoughtful suggestion. It is paradoxical that, in the territory in Africa which is nearest to having an even balance of whites and Africans, there may be the least dialogue. The writer, in fact, made this comment to Chief Hosea Kutako, sitting in council, and it was acknowledged by the usual mumbled "ums" and "ahs" which pass for affirmation.

CONCLUSION

The year 1967 saw the almost final unification of white South Africa growing out of dynamic changes in Afrikaner and English relationships, combined with threats from abroad. An isolationist laager mentality may have given way to a positive and dynamic reaching out. The inclusion of the non-white minorities within the laager is likely, but the government has not gone very far, in specific terms, to include Asian and Coloured citizens. Devolution of power within some federal system or by means of independent Bantu nations may have moved off the drawing board, but the prototypes need testing and separate development is not in regular production or even a proven success in any one instance.

The new foreign policy, while built upon changing racial and political attitudes among white voters, has not resulted in a concomitant change in domestic legal restrictions upon Africans. For example, the generous and much appreciated gift of grain to Lesotho has not meant any change in the amount of general revenue devoted to African education within the Republic, despite the growth in African population and the greater numbers seeking primary and secondary education.

The concept of the Transkei has changed considerably in the public's mind. Adaptations have included far greater latitude than initially planned for the Transkei. The admission of "white capital" is a striking example of modification of the original planning. But in South Africa per se, legal changes have not followed the indications of attitudinal changes.

While unification of the whites makes possible a radically new South African foreign policy, and while some early victories have been achieved, the policy is still far too new to be judged a success or a failure.

Finally, South Africa's ruling white minority is undergoing dynamic change. To think of internal or external policies solely in terms of 1948 or 1958 is to be hopelessly out of date. The fact that there is change, it must be stressed, is no guarantee it will be for the better or for the worse. There are grounds for optimism and for pessimism.

South Africa's future is fluid, evolving, unclear. The input from its own racial minorities and majority, from its African neighbors, from its new friends and many enemies abroad, will play a significant role not only in the future destiny of the whites in South Africa but also, because of their binary relationship, in the future of the African peoples.

The Political Situation

of Non-Whites

in South Africa [1]

―≺✧≻―

Leo Kuper

Racial and ethnic differences are the basis of most of the political divisions within South African society, and they profoundly influence political ideologies. The main political divisions are between whites and non-whites, and politics are essentially politics of race relations. The political ideologies of non-whites may place an ideological emphasis on a broad interracialism, including all the peoples of South Africa; or more narrowly, they may emphasize non-white unity, or African nationalism, or, most narrowly of all, ethnic or tribal identity. These ideological emphases vary with the political situation of different non-white groups and with the changing conditions of South African society, but always the central concern is with race relations.

In this paper I analyze the political situation and ideologies of non-whites as they are affected by racial and ethnic factors under changing economic and social conditions. The first section offers a brief historical review of non-white political movements. The second deals with the main ideological tendencies as they emerge from this historical review. The third relates contemporary political

―――

[1] In preparing this paper I have drawn on a study of African nationalism I have recently completed for a *History of South Africa,* which is being edited by Leonard M. Thompson and Monica Wilson, and is to be published by the Oxford University Press.

movements and ideologies to the political, economic, and social structure of South African society, and raises several questions for discussion.

I: HISTORICAL REVIEW

Concentration of power in the hands of whites and retention of political initiative by whites have dominated the political history of South Africa. There has been a dialectical relationship between white and non-white political power. As more power was assumed by whites—through changes in the franchise, the creation of new structures of control, the introduction of further penal sanctions, and increases in police and military strength—so the power of non-whites—in terms of parliamentary participation, freedom of political association, and the right to oppose state policies—correspondingly diminished. There is a consistent trend in this process from the time of Union. The result has been a monopoly of political power by whites. Non-whites have virtually ceased to be agents of constitutional political action and have become objects of political control: they have been removed from the sphere of politics and active involvement in the affairs of the state to the sphere of administration by government departments.

For Africans, the major events in this consistent contraction of political rights were the South Africa Act of 1910, the Natives Land Act of 1913, the Representation of Natives Act of 1936, and, from 1948, the implementation of apartheid policies. The Act of Union retained the existing Cape African franchise, but at the same time made it explicitly vulnerable to abrogation by a two-thirds majority of the houses of Parliament, and it continued the effective disenfranchisement of Africans in the other provinces. The Natives Land Act of 1913 maintained, in the allocation of scheduled areas for African reserves, the grossly unequal division of land resulting from conquest and dispossession. The Representation of Natives Act of 1936 removed Cape African voters from the common roll and limited African parliamentary representation to three elected white members for the Cape and four elected white senators for the

Union as a whole. Apartheid legislation and policies now seek to revive tribalism. The government has abolished elected parliamentary representation, it has suppressed political opposition, and it has closed the avenues for evolutionary change to a democratic society. All these steps have been taken, moreover, during a period of decolonization and emancipation of oppressed peoples throughout the world.

The Coloureds had never enjoyed the franchise in the northern provinces of the Transvaal and the Orange Free State, but they did exercise the franchise in the Cape and Natal. These franchise rights were adversely affected, prior to apartheid, by the extension of universal adult franchise to whites and by provisions for challenging the registration of non-European voters. Under apartheid, Coloured voters in the Cape were removed from a common roll to communal representation by four white representatives in the House of Assembly in terms of the Separate Representation of Voters Act of 1951 and the South Africa Act Amendment Act of 1956. This was certainly a severe blow, but probably less crucial for Coloureds than compulsory racial categorization under the Population Registration Act of 1950, the decline in civic status by a sort of *gleichschaltung* with Africans, and closure against mobility into the upper racial stratum of South African society.

Indians live in a precarious state of continuing crisis, with occasional remissions. In the last few years, they have been recognized by the government as an integral part of South African society, but their acceptance remains ambivalent. They were disenfranchised in Natal prior to Union, and enjoyed the right to the franchise only in the Cape. For a brief period they were offered a very restricted representation, largely modeled on that devised for Africans, as compensation for compulsory segregation under the Asiatic Land Tenure and Indian Representation Act of 1946. The major peaks in this Indian state of continuing crisis have been restrictions on immigration and trade; compulsory segregation in education, residence, and trade; and outbreaks of extreme racism. The last includes anti-Indian agitation by the English in Natal prior to and during World War II; the attacks under apartheid, seemingly directed in the first decade against the very survival of Indians in South Africa; and the riots of Africans against Indians in Durban in 1949.

As a result of the control of political power by whites, non-white political action has been essentially defensive. Major events in African political activity are clearly related to legislative attacks on African rights. The founding of the African National Congress in 1912 was a response to white initiative in the establishment of the Union of South Africa. The unsuccessful deputations to England in 1914 and again at the end of World War I were a reaction to the Natives Land Act. The Defiance of Unjust Laws Campaign of 1952 was directed toward the repeal of specific laws, though it was conceived as part of a broader strategy for democratic rights. There were certainly periods of militant action, but it is not easy to point to campaigns in which non-whites dictated the issues and exercised the initiative. This is in contrast to the position outside South Africa where Africans, Indians, and Coloureds have taken the initiative in attacks on the government of South Africa at the United Nations and other international forums.

In view of the extreme disparity in numbers between the racial groups, the success of whites in maintaining and strengthening their control of political power has often surprised outside observers. It is less surprising if one remembers that the disparity in numbers is also a disparity between an increasingly well-armed minority and a disarmed majority: Africans were disarmed in the wars of conquest and dispossession, and non-whites have been effectively denied access to arms. In any event, the comparison of numbers is quite misleading. It is based on the invalid assumption that non-whites constitute a unit, and that the sum of their numbers is politically meaningful. In fact there are cultural and language differences between Africans, Indians, and Coloureds, and among Africans themselves, and differences in material conditions and regional location, which impede cooperation. It is necessary to recall the initial distribution of peoples and their varied social, economic, and political situation at the time of Union in order to understand the relative insignificance of non-white numbers in the political history of South Africa.

Differences in the regional location of the racial and ethnic groups were associated with differences in economic role and political rights. Coloureds were concentrated in the Cape, there being only small numbers of Coloureds in the other provinces. They were thus a largely enfranchised population, though few Coloureds in fact exercised the franchise. Their economic role was entirely subordinate, and many were culturally assimilated to whites.

Indians, by contrast, were concentrated in Natal; there were some Indians also in the Cape and the Transvaal, but almost none in the Orange Free State, their entry into that province being prohibited, save for certain specified purposes. Indians were thus mainly subject to the racially repressive policies of the English settlers in Natal, and they were a largely disenfranchised population. They had arrived initially under indenture, being joined later by free or passenger Indians, and they soon entered into competition with whites, who responded by a series of discriminatory laws.

Africans were distributed throughout the Union, but the tribal groups were concentrated in different regions, and there was variation in their relationship to the land, which was the original basis of their subsistence, and in their enjoyment of civic rights. In the *Cape* were concentrated the Xhosa. African tribal settlements were mainly confined to the Transkei, the largest area of continuous African settlement in South Africa. Education for Africans was more advanced in the Cape than in other areas of the Union. There was no legal discrimination in eligibility for the franchise, but only a minority of Africans qualified for the vote, and the qualifications were raised in 1892. The effect of these conditions was therefore to create in the Cape a Western-educated African political elite, with distinctive status and interests.

In *Natal* (including Zululand) were concentrated the Zulu people. African settlement was dispersed, following the dismemberment of the Zulu kingdom, the distribution of Zulus in reserves in Zululand and Natal, and fragmentation under a system of indirect rule. Large numbers were also living on the land of white farmers. Though in theory there was no discrimination in the exercise of the franchise, in practice Africans were effectively disenfranchised. Their legal position was different from that of other groups, since they were made subject to their own customary laws, but there was provision for exemption from Native Law. This encouraged the formation of an educated elite of the exempted, many of whom served white administrators, educators, and missionaries in an auxiliary role.

In the *Orange Free State*, there were mainly Tswana. Most Africans were dispersed on the land of white farmers, there being only two very small reserves. Africans, like Coloureds and Indians, were debarred from exercising the franchise, as they were also in the *Transvaal*. In this province were concentrated Tswana, Southern Sotho, and Pedi: there were also many Africans from a number of Nguni groups. The goldfields were already attracting workers to the Witwatersrand, which was to become the main area for industrial development and intertribal contact. Shortly after Union about one fourth of the Transvaal African population was in the towns, almost one half on farms owned by whites, and the remainder on small reserves, mission stations, and Crown land.

Clearly these conditions to a great extent imposed regional and racially exclusive forms of political organization on non-whites and greatly impeded Union-wide cooperation. Even where national organizations were established, regional factionalism was often a recurrent problem. The growth of African nationalism was dependent on a level of industrialization which would bring together, under similar conditions of living, large numbers of urbanized Africans from different regions and tribal groups. Effective political cooperation between the non-white groups was similarly dependent on these economic and social changes. This level of urbanization and industrialization was not really attained until after World War II. Meanwhile the racial groups developed their own political organizations, and pursued separately their specific interests, though with some intermittent cooperation.

Indians pioneered civil disobedience under the leadership of Mahatma Gandhi. They established the Natal Indian Congress in 1894 and launched the first civil disobedience campaign in 1906–8 against the carrying of registration certificates by Indians in the Transvaal. Resistance continued for some years, with a small measure of success, as a result of the intervention of the British government and the government of India, itself under the British Raj. The link with India continues to be significant, and for many years it had the effect of detaching Indians from any close political association with Africans and Coloureds. Active cooperation only developed after World War II in an alliance of Congresses. Two political tendencies then became manifest in the Indian community, a conservative accommodation toward whites, represented by the South African Indian Organization, and a radical commitment to joint political action with Africans in the South African Indian Congress.

Coloureds established in 1902 an active political body, the African Political Organization, with branches in the Cape, the Transvaal, and the Orange Free State. The exercise of the franchise channeled much of the political participation of Coloureds in support of the white political parties, but Coloureds were active in promoting non-white unity in the Non-European Unity Movement established in 1943. Political activity among Coloureds then became polarized in policies of cooperation with whites, represented by the Coloured People's National Union, and of noncooperation, in the Non-European Unity Movement. Coloured participation in the alliance of racial congresses was, however, of little significance.

For Africans, the basic political problem was to create a national organization which would unify the tribal groups and promote African parliamentary representation and racial equality. The African National Congress was founded for these purposes; inevitably under the conditions of South African society in the first decades after Union, it became a small elite organization. Political action was mainly in the form of petitions and deputations, though there was a civil disobedience campaign in Johannesburg against the Pass Laws in 1919. This followed the pattern of Gandhi's campaign in 1906–8, which greatly influenced Africans, as has been shown in a series of campaigns: in 1913, by African women in Bloemfontein and other towns in the Orange Free State; in 1930, by the Communist Party in Durban; in 1952, by the Congress Alliance; and in 1960, by the Pan-Africanist Congress.

The activities of the African National Congress were overshadowed in the 1920s by a workers' movement, the Industrial and

Commerical Workers Union of Africa, and the Congress declined almost to the point of extinction. It was revived by African reaction against the Representation of Natives Act of 1936 and by the movements for national liberation during and after World War II. In terms of mass following among Africans and of interracial cooperation, the Congress attained its maximum effectiveness in the 1950s. This was as a member of a Congress Alliance committed to interracial political cooperation for the attainment of a common and democratic society. The very strength of this interracial cooperation, as manifested in the Congress of the People in 1955, generated a reaction among Africans and contributed to the founding of the Pan-Africanist Congress in 1959, with an ideology of exclusive nationalism, an anti-Indian platform, and the rejection of any commitment to nonviolence.

In 1960 the African National Congress and the Pan-Africanist Congress were proscribed, and African political activity moved underground. There was a period of sabotage by Umkonto we Sizwe (Spear of the Nation), an offshoot of the African National Congress, and of terrorism by Poqo, an offshoot of the Pan-Africanist Congress, but these organizations were quickly suppressed by the government. At present, there is little evidence of political opposition by Africans inside the country. Outside of South Africa, refugee African political leaders explore the possibilities of international intervention under the complex conditions of the Cold War and of political relations on the African continent.

II: Ideological Tendencies

In discussing non-white political ideologies as they emerge from this brief historical review, it is necessary to deal separately with African ideologies. Ideologies of separatism are potentially more significant among Africans since the Bantustan policies are directed toward the strengthening of tribal identification. Then, too, the position of Africans as a numerical majority in South Africa, on an African continent, is quite distinct from that of the Coloured and Indian minorities. Africans can hope, perhaps realistically, to rule South Africa; Coloureds and Indians must find a *modus vivendi* with the actual and potential ruling groups.

Viewed historically, the major African political ideologies are the following: [2]

I. The ideology of the "Bambata School" that Africans can only regain their freedom on the battlefield where they lost it. The reference is to the Bambata rebellion of 1906, the last armed resistance to the consolidation of conquest and the political subordination of Africans.

II. Ideologies of interracialism, expressed in two different types of organization and political philosophy:

(a) The "Jabavu School," rejecting conceptions of African solidarity and seeking progressive change by interracial political action. The basis of cooperation is participation by individuals, not participation by racial groups. The successors to this school are the Liberal Party and the Progressive Party. The Communist Party shares with these the emphasis on interracial association.

(b) The "Congress School," emphasizing African solidarity as a necessary step toward the sharing of power in a common society. The most complete expression of this ideology was achieved in the Congress Alliance and the Congress of the People. The cooperating units were racially separate Congresses, but the objective was the establishment of a nonracial democratic society. The Communist Party was active in this Alliance, but with some ambivalence toward both African nationalism and the racial basis of the Congress organizations.

III. An ideology of exclusive African nationalism, emphasizing the unique political situation of Africans, rejecting alliance with other racial groups in the struggle, and seeking African majority rule. In common with the ideology of the "Bambata School," there is an emphasis on the necessity of violence to bring about political change. The basis of an exclusive African nationalism in South Africa is race, and not such conventional bases of nationalism as common culture, language, history, and territory. In consequence, this form of nationalism, in a multiracial society, has a strong component of racism.

IV. Ideologies supporting policies of separation. The organizational expression of these ideologies in the past was negligible (as,

[2] See the analysis by J. K. Ngubane in *An African Explains Apartheid* (New York, Frederick A. Praeger, 1961), pp. 69–73.

for example, in the Bantu National Congress), but these ideologies are now encouraged by the Bantustan policies. They may take the form of support for racial separation or for Bantu Authorities or for such limited aspects of racial separation as the exclusion of Indian traders from African areas.

Of these ideologies, that of the "Bambata School," that Africans can only regain their country on the battlefield, was of little significance until the last decade. It was presumably influential in the recent peasant revolts in Pondoland and Zululand and other tribal areas, and in the ideology of exclusive African nationalism.

Sentiments of an exclusive African nationalism were no doubt always present in African political thought, but they only attained significance in organization and action for a brief period inside South Africa. Exclusive nationalism became a realistic political ideology with the achievement of independence by African states and the establishment of Pan-Africanism and of the Organization of African Unity as an international force. The emergence of a militant, exclusive nationalism in South Africa is thus quite recent. The overriding influence in African political thought has been the emphasis on interracialism, though not unmixed with racial antagonisms.

This interracialism of Africans was all the more remarkable in view of the increasing rejection of interracialism in the wider society. Purely strategic considerations no doubt played some part. Racism would certainly have had a stong appeal, but it is based on division, it encourages division, and it might have proved a tenuous basis for uniting the tribal groups. Moreover, if there was to be an effective challenge to government policy, non-white unity must have seemed necessary to mobilize adequate mass support. But these negative considerations were probably of little significance compared to the positive factors inclining Africans toward an affirmation of interracialism. There is a gravitational pull, as it were, toward the interracial core of the society, represented by the urban forms, industrial skills, and educational system introduced from the West, and expressed in innumerable ties of interdependence in an industrializing economy; and there is the attraction for Africans of the values of Western culture, of which one measure may be found in the continuing and increasing affiliation with the mission churches (see table).

Religious Affiliations of Africans in South Africa
in 1911, 1936, and 1960

	1911		1936		1960		Percent of total (all races) denominational affiliation [a]	
	Number (in thousands)	Percent	Number (in thousands)	Percent	Number (in thousands)	Percent	1936	1960
Dutch Reformed	71	1.8	154	2.3	557	5.1	10.9	23.9
Anglican	171	4.2	408	6.2	748	6.9	44.4	53.0
Presbyterian	68	1.7	108	1.6	205	1.9	55.0	63.3
Congregational	96	2.4	57	.8	135	1.2	36.8	46.7
Methodist	452	11.2	795	12.1	1,313	12.0	78.0	77.1
Lutheran	144	3.6	307	4.7	539	4.9	78.3	83.4
Roman Catholic	24	.6	233	3.5	761	7.0	63.6	70.2
Apostolic			13	.2	305	2.8	22.8	63.1
Other Christian	28	.7	63	1.0	508	4.6	35.5	61.8
Bantu Churches			1,089	16.5	2,188	20.1	100.0	100.0
Islam	2	.1	1				1.8	
Other and unspecified	1		38	.6	3,650	33.5	59.9	96.4
No religion	2,962	73.7	3,330	50.5			68.8	
Total [b]	4,019	100.0	6,596	100.0	10,908	100.0		

SOURCE: South Africa, *Population Census, 1960, Sample Tabulation, No. 6*, pp. 2, 16, 25, 29; South Africa, *Union Statistics for Fifty Years*, pp. A-26–A-29.
[a] Not available for 1911 because figures for Coloureds and Asians are not given for that year.
[b] Columns may not add to total because of rounding.

The ideology of interracial cooperation was strongly expressed within the Communist Party of South Africa, and this aspect certainly appealed to many Africans. The Communist Party was also influential in the trade union movement and in the Congress Alliance; but Communism itself never gained a strong following among Africans. This is not easily explained. In Marxist theory, there has been a revolutionary situation for many years in the tension between progressive economic development and increasing political rigidity; or if property relations are viewed in non-Marxist terms, the appropriation of most of the land by whites, and their private ownership of most of the commerical and industrial resources of the country, might have been expected to incline Africans toward Communism. Some of the more important African leaders were dedicated Communists, and mild socialist doctrine was incorporated in the Freedom Charter adopted by the Congress of the People and has appeared in statements by the late President Luthuli of the African National Congress and President Sobukwe of the Pan-Africanist Congress.

For the most part, however, African political leaders have been conservative in their reaction to Communism, or perhaps values in African society have held them back from a commitment to Communism. During two periods in the history of the African National Congress, Communists seemed to be moving toward a dominant position. In the late 1920s there was increasing Communist influence in the Congress, under the presidency of Gumede, and this immediately provoked a strong reaction toward conservative leadership. Again in the 1950s Communist influence in the Congress provoked reaction, and contributed to the secession of the Pan-Africanist Congress, with an anti-Communist ideology. Communism does not seem to have been a significant ideology for Africans. It has attracted neither the main body of African leaders nor the African masses. Class conflicts take the form of racial conflicts, and political radicalism is expressed in ideologies of race relations and not in ideologies of economic relations.

There is one important conception in African political thought which is held by leaders of very different political schools. This is the conception that the structure of white domination in South African society cannot be changed by nonviolent evolutionary means. The evidence for this is derived from interpretations of South African history. Certainly the history of the qualified franchise supports this point of view to some extent. It was a history of the continuous contraction of political rights, and not of an evolutionary expansion of rights. But this is not an inevitable process. There was evolutionary change in the British African colonies, though under conditions in which effective authority was exercised by an outside power. In any event, whether or not the evidence justifies the belief that evolutionary change in white settler societies is an illusion, fostered in the interests of maintaining white domination, the belief is widely expressed by African leaders as a component of their ideologies. This belief is of course associated with the conviction that only violence can bring about change in the structure of South African race relations, and that it is necessary and inevitable.

The ideologies of Indians and Coloureds must be related to their minority position in South African society. The two groups are, however, very different types of minorities. Indians are a scapegoat group with commerical interests coveted by both Afrikaners and Africans, and their minority situation is expressed in a polarization of ideologies between accommodation to whites and identification with Africans. Pressures under apartheid are such as to compel increasing accommodation and cooperation in the segregated institutions of administration and education. The issue is no longer whether to accept or reject segregated Group Areas, but rather that of securing adequate Group Areas for effective survival. Some of the tensions are turned inward in conflicts along lines of religious cleavage and class division, and some security is found in Indian culture and a rich associational life. The interests of Indians are best served by ideologies of interracialism, and they are the most committed, of all the racial groups, to interracial cooperation.

In contrast to Indians, the Coloured minority is an intermediate, and not a scapegoat, group. There have never been attacks against Coloureds, such as were made against Indians, on the grounds that they are foreigners in Africa, alien and unassimilable. Coloureds are acculturated and oriented to whites. The dominant ideology is one of accommodation in a general context of political apathy, but there was a strong and embittered radical ideology, derived from Trotskyism and active in the Non-European Unity Movement. The Unity Movement was committed to non-white unity and to noncooperation with whites in the system of racial domination. Its interpretations of the structure of race relations in South Africa and its prognoses for the future have proved accurate, but the insistence on doctrinal purity has been a source of non-European division rather than unity, and the cause of sharp ideological conflicts in the Coloured community. As long as there was the prospect of Coloureds, or large numbers of Coloureds, being absorbed into the white groups, ideologies of accommodation to whites best corresponded to their material interests. At present, they may be better served by ideologies of interracialism.

III: CONTEMPORARY PERSPECTIVES

Ideologies of interracialism are probably the most widely accepted ideologies among the three non-white groups. Even the more exclusive forms of African nationalism have been obliged to come to terms with the multiracial character of South African society and the rights of its minorities. The declared acceptance as Africans of all persons who identify with Africa and accept the rule of the African majority, the political reclassification of Coloureds as Africans, and the distinctions drawn between working-class and merchant Indians are all attempts to reconcile African nationalism with the multiracial character of South African society.

Ideologies of interracialism are also the most consistent with the economic and social structure of South African society. Processes of change have progressively drawn the racial groups into a common society, with increasing contact and interdependence, as may be seen in statistics of urbanization. The proportion of the population urbanized rose from less than 25 percent immediately after Union to almost 47 percent in 1960 (see Table 9, p. 142). Whites and Asians have become highly urbanized (83 percent), Coloureds appreciably so (69 percent), while the percentage of Africans in urban areas has also risen, even under apartheid, from less than 24 percent in 1946 to 32 percent in 1960. Industry and commerce have increasingly effected an economic integration of the population. There are still large numbers of Africans occupied in subsistence agriculture and migrant labor, and they fall outside the integrated economy or are peripheral to it: but in 1960, about five and a quarter million persons were engaged in the modern sector of the economy, and Africans represented 65 percent of the economically active population.[3] This intermingling of populations continues to increase with sustained economic growth.

Normal processes of change and development in South Africa also encouraged social interaction among members of different groups and fostered a mutual acculturation. There was increasing cooperation in welfare, educational, and sports associations. Africans continued to move into the mission churches, and the great majority of the population of South Africa now shares a common religion, though in many denominational forms and under conditions of extensive segregation. Elements of a common education were beginning to spread more widely through the society, promoting shared interests and a national culture. Now it is precisely these processes of social interweaving and cultural communication that apartheid seeks to reverse: and the strength of these processes may be measured by the large numbers of laws passed to keep the races apart and by the severity of the penal sanctions imposed.

Apartheid may be characterized as a counterrevolution from two points of view. In the first place, it took the form of a centralization of power, with authoritarian structures of control and a resolute use of force. This was represented as necessary to counter a projected revolution, conceived in the form of Communism, as in the Fascist and Nazi counterrevolutions. In the second place, it was counterrevolutionary in its application of the repressive powers of the state to reverse the racially integrative tendencies generated by urbanization and industrialization. As industrialization proceeded, drawing all sections of the population into a common economic structure, so apartheid policy more totally excluded non-whites from political participation and more rigidly petrified racial domination. This is

[3] See D. Hobart Houghton, *The South African Economy* (Cape Town, Oxford University Press, 1964), pp. 205–7.

the essential paradox in the structure of South African society and the context within which the role of non-white political ideologies must be examined. Clearly, under conditions of a virtual monopoly of political power by whites, extensive repression, and the ready use of violence and other extraordinary powers of control, the ideologies of non-whites are likely to be of minor significance within South Africa, unless there are substantial changes in the structure of the situation. The problem becomes one of specifying the changes which might make particular non-white ideologies politically significant.

In the case of interracialism, the model of change generally used involves a process of individuation. Members of different racial groups detach themselves from the racial matrix and enter into relationships across racial barriers, forming the interracial structures of the new society. These increasingly bring about contact on a basis of equality and thus undermine prejudice and release democratizing tendencies. In this process, industrialization is generally regarded as a driving force, since it draws together large numbers of persons of different race in economic interdependence and with rising standards of living, and since industrial efficiency demands selection of personnel by criteria of efficiency and performance. Now South Africa is a vigorously industrializing nation and has been so for at least a generation. Hence the argument is often advanced that industrialization will bring into being a democratic, interracial society, and that the present conflicts are simply the immediate transitional consequences.

There are a number of difficulties in this approach. The most highly industrialized country in the world has by no means resolved its racial conflicts and discriminations, and the level of industrialization in South Africa is quite primitive compared with that of the United States. Moreover, in the United States, American whites and American Negroes share the same political institutions, and progressive changes generated by economic processes can readily become politically effective. In South Africa there are no shared political institutions. As a result, there may be an increasing continuity in the economic structure, reflected in rising wages for non-white workers in the manufacturing industries, greater diversification of occupational opportunities, and growth of professional and commercial strata. At the same time, there may be an increasing rigidity in the political structure, with absolute discontinuity between enfranchised whites and disenfranchised non-whites.

Indeed the competition resulting from industrialization contributes to the increasingly repressive policies of the political system. The white sector of the occupational structure is broadly based, consisting of the many white manual workers and the petite bourgeoisie and lesser bureaucrats. These are the strata most exposed to competition from non-whites and most hostile to any form of non-white political participation. They use their political power to protect themselves against competition and to exclude non-whites. They provide the motive force for the movement under apartheid to greater and greater racial extremism. Some observers see in present developments some abatement of racial extremism. This seems doubtful; in any event, there remain within the National Party the support and leadership for policies of even more extreme racism.

In raising these difficulties, there is no implication that ideologies of interracialism are not highly significant. On the contrary, they arise from the very structure of South African society. The problem, however, is that of envisaging the means by which they could be made effective, and the extent to which these means are available within South African society.

As to ideologies of African nationalism, they are clearly more effective outside South Africa than inside it. Outside the country, in relations with independent African states, the Organization of African Unity, and political interests and powers in the East and the West, there is wide acceptance of African nationalists as the representatives of their people. This acceptance sustains African nationalism and makes it a significant force. Inside the country, African nationalism is at present overwhelmed by the repressive power of the government. But quite apart from political repression, there are elements in the political situation of Indians and Coloureds, and of Africans themselves, which limit the potential effectiveness of African nationalism as a political force.

In analyses of South Africa's racial conflicts, the contending forces are often portrayed as Afrikaner nationalism, or white domination, and African nationalism. Two assumptions are made: first, that Coloureds and Indians may be viewed as assimilated to Africans in the political struggle, and second, that Africans in South Africa are a nation. Neither assumption is correct. Cooperation with Africans is impeded by the situation of Coloureds and Indians as political and demographic minorities, and by differences in culture, political history, geographic distribution, and economic role. In the past, there was rather limited political cooperation with Africans, and that mainly between Indians and Africans in the Congress Alliance in the 1950s, and between Coloureds and Africans in the Non-European Unity Movement in the Cape Province. Today, there is almost no scope for interracial political activity. Moreover, the nationalist ideology of the Pan-Africanist Congress is a rejection of interracial cooperation in the political struggle, and the attacks on Indians in East Africa, under African rule, are no encouragement to cooperation in South Africa. It is quite misleading, in assessing African nationalism, to ignore the distinctive political situation of over two million Indians and Coloureds. Their political interests act as a constraint on the militant forms of African nationalism.

There are restraints also in the structure of African society. Africans, among themselves, must certainly experience sentiments of solidarity and of common identity. In the absence of research, however, it is quite impossible to assess the strength of these sentiments and their significance relative to other identifications, such as with South Africa and its peoples as a whole, or with such ethnic entities as the Swazi, Sotho, Tswana, Xhosa, or Zulu peoples. For leaders of the African National Congress, tribalism was always anathema and always denounced. But given the original distribution and organization of African tribes at the establishment of Union, the policies of succeeding South African governments in maintaining some form of traditional tribal organization, and the character of South African society, it is not surprising that sentiments of tribal identification persist, somewhat fragmenting African nationalism. And African nationalism is further fragmented by divisions between the westernized and the traditional, and between the workers in the towns, the peasants in tribal reserves, and the farm laborers dispersed throughout the country on the land of white farmers. African nationalism is perhaps a potentially effective force, which might have been developed in South Africa either through normal organizational techniques, as the African National Congress attempted, or more expeditiously by violence in the form of a racial civil war.

Meanwhile, the social basis for African nationalism, and for a common interracial society, is in process of change as a result of the implementation of policies of separation under apartheid. Initially these policies stimulated a strong reaction in favor of racial integration. But as the National Party government maintains itself in power, and as its policies are translated into institutional structures and the daily routine of living, much activity is inevitably channeled toward separatism. In the Transkei, the African opposition is committed to a broad South African unity, but it expresses this commitment politically through Bantustan institutions. In Bantu Authorities, in Coloured and Indian advisory committees, in segregated educational institutions, separatism is fostered by activity, and the government is able, in some measure, to weaken the forces both of African nationalism and of interracialism.

Political independence in neighboring African states may similarly divert activity and sentiment. Sections of the many Sotho, Swazi, and Tswana peoples living in South Africa are certain to identify with the new political nation-states of Lesotho, Botswana, and Swaziland, and thereby diminish their active involvement in South African political movements. But at the same time, the independence of these states creates a new structure of race relations in southern Africa and introduces new possibilities of political change. This is probably a highly significant development in terms of new potentialities for change within South African society.

Inside South Africa, the major source of change is likely to be in the tension between the economic and political systems. Presumably, there must be some point at which an equilibrium can no longer be maintained between continued economic growth and increasing political rigidity. At the very least, economic growth must bring about changes in the structure of the groups. Among subordinate groups, elite strata may be expected to renew pressure for political change; and as a result of structural change in the dominant group, there may be some responsiveness among certain strata of whites to these renewed pressures.

Inside southern Africa, there is tension between the international political status of independent African states and the total subjugation of Africans in South Africa. Since many of their people are permanently domiciled in South Africa, and were indeed original inhabitants of the country; and since many of their nationals find employment in South Africa; and since the grounds for the denial of rights to Africans in South Africa are purely racial, the independent African states of southern Africa are inevitably intimately involved in the politics of South Africa. They may be able to exert influence on the government of South Africa for recognition of the basic rights of their peoples, and for restructuring race relations in South Africa.

In the international sphere, there is the tension between a world ethos of racial equality and the South African policy of racial domination, and between doctrines of universal human rights and the systematic negation of these rights in South Africa. The United Nations Organization and other international agencies and associations continue to exert pressure, or seek in other ways, to influence the policies of the South African government. With the creation of independent African states in southern Africa, there may now be more scope for effective action by these international agencies. It may be possible, in cooperation with the independent African states, to introduce changes into the structure of southern Africa in such a way as to stimulate change toward racial equality in the structure of South African race relations under conditions of continued economic growth.

The Case For and Against
United States Disengagement
from South Africa

-<☼>-

William A. Hance

The purpose of this chapter is to examine, primarily from the economic standpoint, the pros and cons of United States disengagement from South Africa. Disengagement is often presented as being intermediate between sanctions, blockade, and war on the one hand and a do-nothing policy on the other. Since disengagement usually represents a stage below sanctions it is first appropriate to indicate why sanctions have tended to be de-emphasized in recent years as an appropriate or acceptable means of bringing down apartheid. That this emphasis may change, however, is noted at the end of Part I.

In Part II an effort is made to suggest what is meant by disengagement, which is defined very differently by various proponents, to indicate the several types or methods of disengagement that have been proposed, and to summarize the reasons that are customarily given for espousing it as an appropriate policy for the United States. The concluding part of this section presents some questions pertaining to the arguments favoring disengagement.

Part III first examines the factual background of U.S. involvement in South Africa. It then turns to the attitudes of American investors and traders with respect to their relations with that country, and concludes with a summary of expressed views regarding their conduct in the Republic.

Claims made regarding the impact of American investment closely parallel those made with respect to the impact of an improving economy in general. It becomes necessary, therefore, to examine certain aspects of the South African demographic and economic scene to assess the validity of these claims, not as to whether the South African economy is aided, which may be taken for granted, but as to whether the non-white is being aided and apartheid is being adversely affected. Focus is upon the black Africans [1] since they comprise the majority of South Africans and space prohibits covering the Coloured and Asian groups.

Part IV, therefore, attempts to assess certain features of the South African scene, including changes in the material welfare of the Africans as measured by employment, wages, and other factors; population growth and distributions by racial groups, which may reveal or lead to a partial failure of apartheid; pressures which have developed to offset influx control and job reservation edicts; and the possibility of the reserve and border industry programs of offsetting the economic pressure on apartheid.

This paper is intended to be as objective as is possible, but it is predicated on the conviction that apartheid is not an acceptable system for human relations. It will receive no defense or support here.

I: THE REDUCTION OF INTEREST IN SANCTIONS

Several years ago there was very considerable interest in the possible application of sanctions [2] as a way of bringing about desired

---

[1] The term African will be used in place of the term Bantu commonly used in South Africa, though it is realized that many persons of other races are also "Africans" by birth, ancestry, or adoption.

[2] For discussions of sanctions against South Africa see: Colin and Margaret Legum, *South Africa: Crisis for the West* (New York, Frederick A. Praeger, 1964); William A. Hance, "Efforts to Alter the Future: Economic Action," in Amelia C. Leiss, ed., *Apartheid and United Nations Collective Measures* (New York, Carnegie Endowment for International Peace, 1965); Ronald Segal, ed., *Economic Sanctions against South Africa* (London, Penguin Books, 1964); U.N. Security Council, Doc. S/6210 (March 2, 1965).

change in South Africa. Some would not agree that there has been a reduction of this interest, but it seems clear that the major powers have rejected sanctions as a method of forcing change in South Africa. The explanations for the lowered interest include the following:

1. doubts regarding the legal justification for sanctions
2. doubts regarding the ability to secure approval for mandatory sanctions in the Security Council
3. doubts regarding the effectiveness of sanctions as a weapon against apartheid:
    a. because of the necessity for universality of application
    b. because historical evidence suggests that sanctions have not been successful, except in time of war. The Taubenfelds have shown that sanctions have been a relatively weak and crude tool, tending to unify opinion in the state against which they were directed and to divide and undermine the international community.[3] Recent experiences with sanctions against Rhodesia and an arms embargo against South Africa have not thus far increased confidence in them. The United States has an impressive record of applying sanctions for moral reasons, but has been less than successful in enlisting widespread support for its actions.
    c. because of factors peculiar to South Africa which would increase the difficulty of applying sanctions, including the juxtaposition of friendly territories, a reasonably high degree of self-sufficiency in the economy, the high value and small bulk of many exports, and the complicating problem of damage to Lesotho, Botswana, and Swaziland
    d. because of the ability of South Africa to offset sanctions by stockpiling, rationing, substitution, preemptive purchasing and allocation of raw materials, extension of labor controls, repatriation of foreign labor, use of equipment beyond its normal life, partial replacement of foreign markets by the domestic market, and possible sale of high-value, nonperishable goods

[3] Rita F. and Howard J. Taubenfeld, "The 'Economic Weapon': The League and the United Nations," *Proceedings of the American Society of International Law* (1964), pp. 183–206.

for future delivery. The Republic has been giving particular attention to offsetting a possible oil embargo,[4] has offered incentives to certain industries to stockpile strategic raw materials, and has promoted the establishment of industries designed to provide strategic items for the South African economy.

4. fears regarding the impact and outcome of sanctions:
   a. on South African whites. An American representative at the U.N. suggested in 1963 that "far from encouraging the beginnings of a dialogue punitive measures would only provoke intransigence and harden the existing situation." Nor could even successful sanctions be expected to destroy the Afrikaner's racial convictions.
   b. on South African non-whites, who might be the most severely damaged instead of being aided. The counterargument that the Africans are prepared to suffer would carry more weight if there were confidence in achieving a reasonably prompt and successful outcome through sanctions.
   c. on such heavily dependent countries as Lesotho, Botswana, Swaziland, Malawi, and even Zambia
   d. on South Africa's major trading partners and investors, particularly the United Kingdom whose economic health and precarious balance of payments could be seriously affected. There is also concern regarding the effect on national and international liquidity of any boycott on gold from South Africa, though some would welcome the opportunity to introduce reforms in international financing.
   e. on the United Nations. Unsuccessful sanctions, it is argued, would lead to disillusion and the erosion of will to take other action, which might prove fatal to the United Nations. Or, in a somewhat contradictory interpretation, unsuccessful sanctions might lead to a call for more forceful measures, thus sparking off a conflict they were intended to avoid. Indeed,

[4] Including a major exploration program, purchase and construction of tankers, increasing the storage capacity (estimated at a two-year supply in April, 1967), construction of a government-owned refinery near Johannesburg, increasing the capacity of the oil-from-coal facilities at Sasolburg, and attempting to conclude agreements for the supply of crude oil irrespective of sanctions.

there is wide acceptance that to be successful sanctions would require imposing a blockade, which is an act of war and which could readily lead to a shooting war.[5] If coercive measures were successful, other doubts arise. Such an outcome might provoke internal disorders, call for the landing of a U.N. force to prevent chaos and massacre, and require the long-term presence of a mediating force. It could start a race war or even a cold-war conflict, both of which sanctions were intended to prevent.

Despite the formidable objections to sanctions it is entirely conceivable that they may sooner or later be adopted. A second Sharpeville or other unpredictable events might unite the world community in acceptance of coercive measures. Success of mandatory sanctions against Rhodesia might bring renewed interest in their application to South Africa. The continued demands of African nations, which have not acceded that sanctions are undesirable or ineffective, might eventually bear fruit.

Another possibility is that sanctions could be accepted and applied as an imperfect weapon, with prior acknowledgment that their impact was not expected to be effective. Such a position would employ sanctions as a moral, not an economic, weapon. It might also be possible to secure more widespread approval of partial sanctions, particularly on the shipment of arms to South Africa.

Finally, it is conceivable that the international community might preplan a sanctioning effort with sufficient skill to offset several of the major objections to it. This might involve an agreement not to impose sanctions until all had agreed to enforce them, until some arrangements had been concluded for compensatory payments, and until contingency planning had been completed for a series of possible outcomes. Such a program would require a higher degree of

[5] Considerations such as this led the British Council of Churches to reject sanctions since they were "not prepared to support a policy which depends upon a calculation as to the relative merits of spilling x or y pints of human blood, anyway as long as there is any conceivable alternative." British Council of Churches, *The Future of South Africa: A Study by British Christians* (London, SCM Press, 1965), p. 21.

international cooperation and managerial ability than is characteristically manifest.

II: DISENGAGEMENT EXAMINED

It is generally accepted that disengagement is middle ground between sanctions and a do-nothing policy. Unfortunately, however,
it is nowhere clearly defined and there is a considerable degree of
conflict and contradiction in the proposals that have been made regarding disengagement. These proposals comprise a range of steps
from verbal condemnation up to and including sanctions. Some say
that disengagement is passive,[6] others that it is aggressive. To a
few it appears to be sanctions under a different name, but the fact
that it can be unilateral or even personal does distinguish it from
the normal concept of sanctions.

Proponents of disengagement frequently favor a carrot-and-stick
approach, calling on the one hand for a series of positive steps and
on the other for encouraging a dialogue with South Africa or
among racial groups in the Republic. It is sometimes suggested that
a series of disengaging steps of increasing intensity might be an-
nounced and applied *ad seriatim,* thus heightening the psychological impact.

Depending on the measures suggested, disengagement can reflect
a policy of neutralism, noncooperation, dissociation, intervention, or
withdrawal. It can reflect a desire to induce a change in South Africa by positive steps, or an acceptance that little can be done but
that the disengager will at least not be implicated or involved in a
detested situation. To some it is the isolation of the disengager that
is the goal; others appear to be propounding a full-as-possible isolation of South Africa.

Methods or Types of Disengagement

A better concept of the possible meanings of disengagement may
be derived by noting the various measures that have been sug-

[6] See Henry P. Van Dusen, "Disengagement from South Africa," *Wind and
Chaff* (October, 1964).

gested. It must be reiterated, however, that various proponents recommend varying combinations, and that some of those listed are contradictory or mutually exclusive.

First, it is widely proposed that verbal condemnations of apartheid be made by high government officials and that greater initiative be taken by American delegates in censuring motions at the United Nations. Second, various steps are set forth to reduce governmental involvement in South Africa, including removal of the NASA tracking station; cessation of any cooperation with the South Africa Atomic Energy Board; discontinuing any government expenditures or actions to encourage, assist, or guarantee new investment in South Africa; informing potential investors of the dangers of investing in the Republic; recalling commercial and military attachés; recalling the ambassador; and severing all diplomatic relations with South Africa.

Third, measures are suggested that are intended to reduce the economic involvement of the United States. Those applied to capital movements include steps to dissuade or prohibit new investment or to encourage disinvestment. Those applied to trade include the ending of all special trade privileges (e.g., the South African share of the U.S. sugar quota or, for Britain, advantages inherited by South Africa from the Commonwealth), placing a broad range of exports under the Export Control Act, and the cessation of all trade with South Africa. It is also frequently suggested that American companies operating in the Republic be pressed to present a creditable example with respect to wages, fringe benefits, and employee and race relations, and that visiting businessmen be requested to refrain scrupulously from statements which might be exploited by South African propagandists. The bulk of this paper is concerned with assessing the pros and cons of economic disengagement.

A fourth type of disengagement is concerned with personal movements, and includes such measures as the discouragement or banning of tourist travel and permanent emigration to South Africa. The latter has more pertinence to Britain and some of the continental European countries. A fifth type involves the ending or drastic reduction of cultural contacts, including visits of musicians, artists, and athletes, and the insistence on reciprocity in public and private exchange programs. It is suggested by some that official protests be lodged if the Republic refuses to permit selected Africans and other South Africans to visit the United States or selected Americans to visit that country.

Last, it is commonly suggested that the United States adopt or enlarge certain programs outside South Africa that would be seen to be critical of apartheid, including increased aid to refugees from that country and aid to such countries as Lesotho, Botswana, and Malawi to decrease their dependence on the Republic.

Why Disengagement Is Propounded

The major reason given by those who support disengagement as a U.S. policy is the desirability of doing something with respect to an abhorrent system. The British Council of Churches put the case as follows:

If Christians cannot call for a naval blockade, followed by a U.N. expeditionary force, . . . they have to face the challenge what else do they propose? Is the concern for love to exclude the concern for justice, or compassion for the Afrikaner to nullify compassion for the economic helots who are obliged to serve them? [7]

In the same vein the Council study quoted Archbishop Joost de Blank and Bishop Ambrose Reeves as writing that "those who oppose sanctions must put forward some alternative method of bringing home to the South African Government the enormity of their policies." [8] Others have pointed out that appeals to reason have not worked, that authority unquestioned seldom questions itself, and that it is a rare despot who volunteers reform.

The most important arguments given in support of disengagement are based on the uniqueness of the South African situation, the contention that conflict will occur if there is inaction, and the wish to make the United States stance toward apartheid more credible.

[7] British Council of Churches, *Future of South Africa*, p. 78.
[8] *Ibid.*

Waldemar A. Nielsen, president of the African-American Institute, put the matter of uniqueness as follows:

The South African Problem is not just another case of totalitarianism. It is not just another threat to human freedom. It is in addition the most flagrant and clearcut case in the world today of oppression of colored people by white people as a matter of official policy. It is the No. 1 case in the world, therefore, of a threat to human freedom based on race. And race is a factor in world politics of potentially catastrophic proportions.[9]

With respect to the threat of future continental or world conflict, the argument is that we have a moral imperative to act before war breaks out. Not only is it feared that a racial war is threatened on at least a continent-wide basis but it is felt that the South African slag heap contains the seeds of eventual cold-war conflict. And in the latter context it is sometimes suggested (for example, by the Committee on Conscience and the American Committee on Africa) that the United States might tragically be drawn to the defense of the South African government and to fighting against the non-whites in Africa.

American policy, it is further argued, must be made credible in its opposition to racial discrimination and specifically to apartheid. At present the United States is variously seen as "identified with," "involved," "implicated," and "responsible for," or as "partners" or "accomplices" in apartheid.[10] Spoken condemnation is seen as inadequate, since it is not taken seriously in South Africa. The need is to make clear our dissociation from a morally reprehensible policy, particularly to Africans, who see apartheid as "the most abominable symbol of the worst humiliation that the centuries have imposed on Africa." [11] But it is also required vis-à-vis South African whites, on

[9] *United States–South African Relations,* Hearings before the Subcommittee on Africa of the Committee on Foreign Affairs, House of Representatives, Part I (Washington, GPO, 1966), p. 76.

[10] See such sources as: "Partners in Apartheid," *Africa Today* (March, 1964); "A Special Report on American Involvement in the South African Economy," *Africa Today* (January, 1966), which sees a "symbiotic relation between apartheid and certain segments of the American business community"; letters to the New York *Times* from James Farmer (March 16, 1967) and from A. Philip Randolph (December 1, 1966); and U.N. Doc. A/AC.109/L.154 (October 16, 1964).

[11] Secretary-General of the Organization of African Unity, quoted in British Council of Churches, *Future of South Africa,* p. 14.

the one hand to give some encouragement to liberals and on the other to indicate to the government that it could not claim U.S. support and confidence.

Additional reasons given for supporting a policy of disengagement include the desire to prevent damage to the U.N., to raise the cost of apartheid somewhat, and to obviate later embarrassment should South Africa seek to mobilize American branch plants for defense production.

Finally, some proponents see economic disengagement as slowing the rate of economic growth in South Africa and thus threatening "the continuance of the whole system, which is based, in the long run particularly, on a high rate of growth." [12] It is further claimed in support of this thesis that South African prosperity depends on the influx of capital and on the confidence of the international business community, particularly the British and American components.

Questions Regarding the Arguments for Disengagement

The arguments given by the proponents of disengagement require some questioning before a presentation of the factual details of U.S. economic involvement and an assessment of the impact of economic growth on apartheid.

First, a number of questions may be posed regarding U.S. involvement. There is widespread agreement that this country must be concerned with South Africa because of our moral abhorrence of its racial policies, our interest in the U.N., our desire for stability in South Africa, and the cold-war competition for the allegiance of other African peoples. It is also in our national interest, as Vernon McKay has pointed out, to induce South Africa to rid itself of an unworkable policy that can bring only trouble to it and the rest of the world, and to remain true to our principles that just governments are based on the consent of the governed and that we oppose laws anywhere that discriminate against a human being because of the color of his skin.

[12] E. Feit, "Conflict and Cohesion in South Africa," *Economic Development and Cultural Change*, XIV, No. 4 (July, 1966), 495.

But it may be questioned whether an acceptance of concern may fairly be equated with an acceptance of implication in or responsibility for racial affairs in South Africa, either because a majority of Americans are the same color as white South Africans, because the South African government identifies itself as a champion of Western civilization, because the Africans say we are responsible, because the Communists call South Africa our "junior partner," or because the United States maintains diplomatic and commercial relations with the Republic. Nor is it logical to imply that having reservations about the use of coercive measures is tantamount to support of apartheid.

Some observers also query the degree of uniqueness of South African sinning. They suggest that at least half of the members of the U.N. do not have governments clearly based on majority rule, do not adhere to the Charter, or do not practice the basic concepts of human rights. Whatever the validity of this argument may be, its weakness is that nowhere else has racial discrimination been enshrined as an official policy.

It is interesting that the call for more effective action against South Africa comes at a time when there is growing criticism of excessive U.S. commitment around the world and increasing support for achieving détentes with countries that have heretofore been ostracized. Senator Fulbright writes of *The Arrogance of Power*. Hans Morgenthau opines that "we have come to overrate enormously what a nation can do for another nation by intervening in its affairs" and that if national interests and available power were more carefully calculated the United States would "intervene less and succeed more." [13] Senator Javits states that the more contact China has the more likely it will become a responsible power and that this is especially important before it becomes a nuclear power. Henry Steele Commager writes:

It is not our duty to keep peace throughout the globe . . . to stop the advance of Communism or other isms which we may not approve of. . . . Would it not be wise . . . if we used our immense power and resources to wipe out poverty and injustice and waste at home before

[13] Hans J. Morgenthau, "To Intervene or Not to Intervene," *Foreign Affairs* (April, 1967), pp. 435–36.

launching ourselves upon crusades to wipe out these things in distant continents? [14]

A number of questions also arise regarding the credibility of the U.S. stance. Some observers have suggested, for example, that respect for America will be based far more upon what is done with regard to our domestic racial problems than upon what is done in South Africa. Others have questioned whether Africans give as high priority to South Africa as is often claimed and whether the West should, in any case, accede that South Africa has such overriding significance. Dennis Austin put the case as follows with respect to Britain and South Africa:

To portray the African states as strongly united within the OAU, and uniformly hostile to Britain because of its reluctance to endorse extreme measures against South Africa, is to portray a phantom . . . relations with the west are both good and bad according to the context in which they are examined.[15]

Still others have opined that the United States must be careful to determine its policies on the basis of its own national interests, which may or may not coincide with what is demanded by Africans. Some concern has also been expressed as to whether disengagement would be adequate to sustain the credibility of the U.S. stance, since Africans are likely to demand more coercive action if disengagement does not have the desired effect.

A third type of question regarding disengagement has to do with the possible costs of various measures to the United States and its allies, particularly if their place is simply assumed by other nations. Any assessment of the potential costs of U.S. disengagement requires a knowledge of our present economic involvement, which is presented in the following section.

The effectiveness of disengagement has also been questioned on a variety of grounds. Some observers fear that it would simply make South African nationalists more xenophobic and more resistant to change than they already are. Some have suggested that

[14] Henry Steele Commager, "How Not to Be a World Power," *The New York Times Magazine* (March 12, 1967), p. 28 ff.

[15] Dennis Austin, *Britain and South Africa* (London, Oxford University Press for the Royal Institute of International Affairs, 1966), p. 56.

South Africa would be aided because it would just intensify its efforts to achieve self-sufficiency.[16] And others have suggested that, since there is considerable doubt regarding the effectiveness of sanctions, there must be greater doubt regarding the ability of lesser measures to effect a change.

Additional doubts pertain to those measures which would tend to reduce contacts between South Africans and the West. If such measures were adopted, the ability to carry on a dialogue would be decreased, whereas many would subscribe to the need for a wide variety of cultural and scientific contacts intended to combat the tendency of South Africa to drift into sterile isolation. A case can be made, in fact, that it was a mistake to give South Africa cause to withdraw from UNESCO, ECA, FAO, and ILO, and to suspend its voting privilege in WHO. At a time when there is increasing support for the admission of Mainland China to the U.N. it does not appear sensible to expel or to encourage the withdrawal of South Africa. As the U.S. delegate stated in the Security Council in 1963, "As for suggestions of diplomatic isolation, persuasion cannot be exercised in a vacuum. Conflicting views cannot be reconciled *in absentia.*"

Insofar as disengagement is seen as a policy which cleanses the initiator by a discontinuance of contact, it is difficult to see how a positive achievement would result. Dennis Austin commented in this regard as follows:

Apartheid is an evil, but neither Britain nor the United States—nor western Europe—has the right to wash its hands of the responsibility for what may happen. . . . By refusing to isolate South Africa . . . the west may be able to sustain hope among those who not only refuse to accept apartheid, but who keep alive the possibility of peaceful change.[17]

Next, there are several questions regarding the outcome and the impact of disengagement. Many of the concerns are identical to

[16] Much too much has probably been made of the supposedly increasing self-sufficiency of the Republic. It is true that there has been promotion of import substitution, as there would be in any developing economy, but the growth and increasing sophistication of the economy has made South Africa "crucially dependent on raw materials and intermediate supplies" for a number of expanding industries. Quote from *The Economist* (December 10, 1966), p. 1161.

[17] Austin, *Britain and South Africa*, p. 23.

those expressed with respect to sanctions, noted in Part I of this paper: Will the South African government be sufficiently affected to induce a change? Will South African non-whites bear the major brunt of any impact? [18] Is it not possible that apartheid will be strengthened and that the chances for increasing economic integration will be lessened by whatever impoverishment is achieved, or by weakening those forces which are now working against apartheid? Is there a better chance for a favorable outcome in the long run with or without economic integration? If the outcome of disengagement is the isolation of the United States from South Africa may we not have opted for a policy of inertia and despair? Some of the matters examined in Part IV have pertinence to these questions.

Finally, a number of questions have been raised regarding the propriety of certain of the suggested types of disengagement and of some of the tactical methods employed in its support. First is the question whether business should be expected to adopt political policies which have not yet been set by the government; this is briefly examined in Part III. Second is the question whether the attack on apartheid has not been partially misdirected into an attack on American business and on the free enterprise system in general, thus to some extent splitting the ranks if not obfuscating the issue.

It may also be asked whether trade should be so readily proposed as a potential weapon, whether, in fact, it has not already been grossly overworked in a variety of situations and with consistently ineffectual results. The traditional argument of trading nations that, except in times of war, markets and goods are neutral, and that one trades neither with friends nor enemies but with customers, still has validity. Nor can one welcome the proliferation of actual or threatened trade sanctions, whether they be unilateral or not. Consider the existing sanctioning efforts against Israel, Cuba, North Vietnam, China, and others, the threatened sanctions against Britain and the United States if they do not sanction South Africa,

---

[18] In a letter sent to 30 American business leaders in early 1967 Senator Robert Kennedy expressed his objection to financial disengagement because "the cost to non-whites might far outweigh any change in that government's policies."

or the various sanctioning programs emanating from the Arab-Israeli war of 1967.

Lastly, the question may be asked with respect to a number of the disengaging methods: Are we in danger of catching the virus, of responding to illiberalism by adoption of illiberal measures ourselves? Such a question applies to the support of isolation rather than concern, the suggested interference with tourist and other movements to South Africa, or the notion that somehow all Americans commenting on South Africa should reflect an approved line.

In this section certain questions have been posed regarding the arguments for disengagement. Some have been discussed briefly; some probably have no answer except in time; the information presented in the following parts may hopefully contribute to answering a number of the others.

III: UNITED STATES ECONOMIC INVOLVEMENT
WITH SOUTH AFRICA

Measures of the Involvement

Investment. According to data supplied to the O'Hara Committee by the government, there are some 237 U.S. subsidiaries, affiliates, and branch offices in South Africa. American firms control half or more of the capital of 78 percent of this group and less than half of the capital of about 8 percent; 10 percent are primarily service branches; and the remaining 4 percent are owned by resident Americans. The nationality of the executives is divided approximately as follows: 43 percent, South African; 37 percent, American; 11 percent, British; and 9 percent, other, mostly Western Europeans.[19]

United States private direct investment in the Republic totaled $528 million in 1965, which was 1.1 percent of total foreign investments. Investment in South Africa has grown at about the same rate as total foreign investments. Most of the U.S. investment in South Africa has been financed by retained earnings, less than one third coming from fresh capital inflows. In the period 1961–65 new capi-

---

[19] *United States–South African Relations,* Part I, pp. 15–26.

tal moving to the Republic averaged $13 million a year but increased steadily to $30 million in 1965. New money from this country is less important to U.S. investment in South Africa than to U.S. investment as a whole. In 1961–65 Africa took 6.3 percent of fresh U.S. direct investment; South Africa took 0.9 percent.

The rate of return of U.S. direct investment in South Africa has been consistently high, averaging 19.5 percent in the period 1961–65. Repatriated dividends and profits on direct investment have, in fact, persistently exceeded the U.S. net capital outflow to that country.

There has been a relative decline of U.S. investment in mining and a relative increase of investment in manufacturing in recent years; manufacturing substantially outranks other sectors, accounting for 44.9 percent of total U.S. investment in South Africa in 1965.

While the importance of our investments in and financial transactions with South Africa is quite minor in relation to total U.S. foreign transactions, they play a more significant role for South Africa. At the end of 1965 the United States ranked second among holders of the Republic's foreign liabilities with 11.8 percent of the total; the United Kingdom is by far the largest holder (58.8 percent) and Western Europe as a whole outranks the United States with a total of 16.3 percent. In the private sector the United States accounted for 12.2 percent ($492 million) of the total and the U.K. for 61.7 percent.

But South Africa had an excess of domestic savings over investment in 1961–65, so that savings generated within the country were more than sufficient to finance gross investments. In 1964 and 1965, however, gross domestic investment exceeded savings by $458 million, which was financed by reducing external reserves by $175 million and by importing, in 1965 only, capital in the amount of $283 million. In 1965 net capital inflow represented 12.6 percent of gross domestic savings, a not inconsiderable amount.

In the ten-year period 1956–65 the private sector (excluding banks) in South Africa invested abroad and/or reduced its foreign liabilities by a total of $428 million, while the government-banking sector was a net importer of foreign capital by a total of $176 million. However, the South African private sector was a net importer of *direct* investments during this period by about $155 million and a large-scale net exporter of portfolio capital, owing mainly to a substantial decline in foreign holdings of South African securities. In its total balance of indebtedness South Africa appears to be moving gradually toward a net creditor position.

This suggests that the qualitative aspects of American investment, particularly in manufacturing because of the innovating character of some portion of it, may be of greater significance than the dollar flow of investment capital. And U.S. Investment in manufacturing is more important to the Republic than our investment in other sectors; in the period 1961–65 American afflliates accounted for nearly 10 percent of fixed investment expenditures in manufacturing and construction in the Republic, and in 1965 U.S. manufacturing affiliates accounted for roughly 8–10 percent of total sales by the manufacturing industry in South Africa.

Trade Relations. South Africa ranked in 1965 as the fourteenth customer for U.S. exports and the eighteenth supplier of its imports. In 1966 the Republic took 1.3 percent of the total value of U.S. exports (Table 1); the 1966 level represented about 30 percent of U.S. exports to Africa. If trade between the two nations were interrupted, the impact on U.S. exports would not be particularly important though some difficulty would doubtless be faced in securing alternative markets for a portion. An estimated 50,000 persons were employed in the United States in 1963 in producing goods sold to South Africa.

U.S. imports from South Africa are about 1 percent of total imports by value with some decline having occurred in their relative significance from 1962 to 1966. The impact of a ban on imports from South Africa might be most important qualitatively for certain grades of asbestos, platinum, gem diamonds, chemical chrome, and wool, though in no case would it result in serious difficulties. Uranium oxide has ranked as the number one import in recent years, but its value declined considerably in 1964 and 1965 owing to fulfillment of contracts. Even if a unilateral cessation of trade occurred, many minerals and metals from South Africa would doubtless find their way to this country via third-party countries.

TABLE 1

Selected Data on South African Trade, 1958–1966

South Africa

Year	Total exports (in million $)	Percent to U.S.	Percent to U.K.	Total imports (in million $)	Percent from U.S.	Percent from U.K.
1958	1,097	7.2	31.2	1,557	7.7	33.7
1959	1,200	9.3	30.2	1,368	19.9	31.1
1960	1,226	6.7	30.8	1,555	18.9	28.4
1961	1,325	8.3	32.9	1,401	17.7	29.2
1962	1,333	9.0	30.5	1,436	16.5	30.3
1963	1,386	9.0	32.4	1,698	16.8	29.8
1964	1,459	8.5	32.8	2,150	19.0	28.2
1965	1,427	8.2	36.8	2,261	19.4	33.1
1966	1,688	11.3	33.1	2,307	17.7	27.3

United States

Year	Total exports (in million $)	Percent to S.A.	Percent to rest of Africa	Total imports (in million $)	Percent from S.A.	Percent from rest of Africa
1958	17,904	1.7	2.0	13,410	1.5	3.4
1959	17,645	1.3	2.6	15,697	1.3	3.0
1960	20,587	1.3	2.3	15,065	1.3	2.8
1961	20,998	1.1	2.8	14,756	1.4	3.1
1962	21,687	1.0	3.5	16,457	1.6	3.0
1963	23,386	1.2	4.1	17,213	1.5	3.0
1964	26,631	1.5	3.0	18,751	1.3	3.5
1965	27,401	1.6	2.8	21,432	1.1	3.0
1966	30,450	1.3	3.0	25,629	1.0	2.8

SOURCE: International Monetary Fund, *Direction of Trade,* various issues.

Trade with the United States is considerably more important to South Africa. The United States accounted for 17.7 percent [20] of total South African imports and about 11.3 percent of its exports in

[20] There are substantial discrepancies in trade figures issued by the International Monetary Fund, the U.N., and South African and U.S. sources. These probably reflect differences in recording shipments of classified material (e.g., uranium oxide) and in classifying imports and exports by source and destination.

1966. Imports from the United States have tended to rise more rapidly than exports to this country.

Gold. The movement of nonmonetary gold from South Africa more than offsets the deficit in physical trade, though the surplus of exports plus gold over imports narrowed sharply in 1964 and 1965 owing to large increases in imports. A unilateral economic disengagement from South Africa by the United States would have no discernible impact on gold sales.

Balance of Payments. If there were a total cessation of American–South African economic relations the loss to the U.S. balance of payments has been estimated at an initial $250 million for trade and $50 million for invisible earnings. This may be small in relation to total U.S. external transactions; it does have somewhat greater significance in relation to the existing balance of payments position. The Department of Commerce has estimated that South Africa supplies about 4 percent of our global trade surplus though it accounts for less than 2 percent of our total trade by value.

Impact on the United Kingdom. Probably more significant than any direct impact of economic disengagement on the United States would be the indirect effects on this country if the United Kingdom were also to follow such a policy. The dependence of Britain on its economic relations with South Africa is much greater than that of the United States,[21] and a severance of these relations [22] in face of

---

[21] About 5 percent of U.K. exports go to South Africa and 3 percent of imports come from that country. Earnings from investments have been about $170 million a year. Earnings on shipping, tourism, insurance, and other services have been about $112–140 million a year. Britain accounted for 58.9 percent of total South African foreign liabilities in 1965. Total economic disengagement would worsen the balance of payments by an estimated $840 million in the first year. See U.N. Doc. S/6210; *Africa Digest* (February, 1967), pp. 78–79; and Austin, *Britain and South Africa,* pp. 146–47.

[22] Even a threat of unilateral sanctions could have a serious impact, as is indicated by the South African reaction when Lloyds was forced to renege on its Rhodesian commitments. The Republic then amended its insurance law to require Lloyds' underwriters to maintain deposits in that country equal to 70 percent of local premiums. There has also been talk in South Africa of possibly bypassing the London gold market. And South Africa would also doubtless move to secure alternative sources of imports before trade sanctions were applied.

a somewhat precarious balance of payments position might require some substantial rescue operations by other nations and especially by the United States. If the United States were to consider a uni-lateral economic disengagement from South Africa it would be in a delicate position with respect to the British position, for it would wish neither to use its concern for Britain as an excuse for not adopting the policy, nor to put that country on the spot by taking action which would greatly increase pressure on Britain to do the same.

The Attitudes of American Business Involved in South Africa

United States investors and traders doing business in South Af-rica have generally been reluctant to make public statements re-garding their position, in part because such expressions are usually demanded by hostile audiences which are unlikely to examine the issues dispassionately. This section attempts to summarize the gen-eral attitudes of American businessmen with respect to the criticism of their relations with South Africa.

First, investors state that it is the business of the State Depart-ment to determine foreign policy, that private enterprise should not be called upon to form such policy, to substitute for government inaction, or to impose private economic sanctions when official sanc-tions have not been legislated. The official policy of the govern-ment is that it "neither encourages nor discourages" American in-vestment in South Africa. The potential investor is briefed if he seeks advice "on the political and racial situation, the outlook in the Republic, and American policies and interests," but "the decision about whether to invest remains with the individual or company." [23]

Business, it is further argued, must essentially be neutral in a for-eign country. Being guests within that country, businessmen must be sensitive to the local mores and laws and must use discretion in their dealings with local citizens and government officials. The va-lidity of this argument is suggested by the necessity of the large oil companies to operate in a multitude of producing and consuming

[23] *United States–South African Relations,* Part I, p. 8.

countries, many of whose official policies are subject to serious objections. These companies have found it essential to adopt the policy that for them "business knows no politics."

There is also justification for the claim that investors would be strongly criticized for assuming the State Department's functions if they were seen to be interceding in the domestic politics of almost any nation other than South Africa, and hence that those who call upon them to disengage are applying a double standard and asking them to do the same.

It follows from the above that investment should not be taken as indicative of support of any country's social, political, or economic policies. Because South Africa claims that American or British investment implies support of that country does not make it so, and such claims should not induce a reaction on our part that was not justified on other grounds.[24] We cannot control what South Africans say or believe; this can only be offset by reiterating our rejection of apartheid and our concern that this policy entails grave dangers for the future well-being of the country.

A number of American businesses have reacted to the criticism of their relations with South Africa by noting that they do attempt to improve conditions when they are able, as is indicated by their achievements at home and in other countries.[25] Their ability to effect change varies enormously from country to country and they

[24] Not all South Africans see foreign investment as supportive. The Deputy Minister of Labour said in late 1963: "The enemies of South Africa are prepared to encourage foreign investors to invest as much as they can because they consider every dollar invested will crack and destroy what they believe to be the myth of apartheid." (Quoted in Christopher R. Hill, *Bantustans: The Fragmentation of South Africa* [London, Oxford University Press, 1964], p. 20.) Nationalist businessmen have also pointed to the dangers of foreign control over the two big banks, Barclays and Standard. A study is reported to have been made in 1966 by the Department of Finance of ways in which control could be transferred to South African shareholders, but, according to *The Economist* (November 26, 1966), p. 942, "it looks very much as though this was found to be impractical."

[25] Examples include the successful action of American Metal Climax through the Rhodesian (now Roan) Selection Trust in ending the discriminatory color bar on the Zambian copper mines in 1956, pioneering by the First National City Bank in the employment of minority groups in the United States, and participation by many of the firms in developing countries throughout the world and particularly in Africa. These actions, it is maintained, help to accomplish the goal of dissociation from apartheid.

often face the very delicate task of conducting themselves in such a way that they would be accepted by whatever the successor government might be. In South Africa the ability of foreign investors admittedly is sharply limited by the proliferation and massiveness of repressive legislation, which all the companies together could not end.

Private interests also point to the difficulties of withdrawing investment from South Africa or even of discontinuing to maintain their existing investments, most of which were made at a time when no stigma was attached to investing in that country. Physical plants such as a factory or a mine cannot be withdrawn; some could not be sold without considerable loss at knockdown or fire-sale prices. And, unless one assumes that the conduct of American business in South Africa is below average in its commitment to improving conditions and human relations, there would likely be some loss to employees of all racial groups. Furthermore, both mining and industry require continuing investment either to replace depleting reserves, to maintain and improve the existing product and the competitive position of the investor, or to sustain the existing investment. There are, at the same time, restrictions on the full repatriation of earnings, and most companies would prefer to invest these retained earnings in their own endeavors. Finally, the adoption of certain disengaging measures could lead to the nationalization of American-owned properties and assets in South Africa.

American investors also often claim that their investment contributes to the weakening of apartheid, that disinvestment would not bring the economy to a halt, and that a campaign of disengagement would most harm those whom it was intended to aid. Since the arguments for these claims are the same as those given with respect to the favorable impact of a burgeoning economy, their examination is more appropriate to Part IV of this study.

The Conduct of American Business in South Africa

Those favoring economic disengagement from South Africa have frequently argued that American business conduct in that country supports the contention that we are "implicated in apartheid." The

American Committee on Africa states, for example, that U.S. companies "operate locally with hardly a murmur." Philip Quigg, who favors discouraging new investment, writes: "For a group which professes to be apolitical, American businessmen in South Africa manage to be extraordinarily articulate in support of apartheid." [26] Others see the image of American business neither as good as it should be nor as it could be even under South African laws, and suggest that British- and even some Afrikaner-owned companies have a more commendable record.

G. Mennen Williams, then assistant secretary of state for African affairs, told the O'Hara Committee on March 1, 1966, that "while American companies operating in South Africa are, of course, obliged to abide by South African laws, we are encouraged by their generally progressive record." [27] Alexander Trowbridge, assistant secretary of commerce for domestic and international business, told the Committee that

the presence of U.S. business in South Africa has, in certain limited areas, exerted a positive influence on some aspects of racial practices in South Africa, particularly in the industrial sphere. In many instances, U.S. firms have been in the forefront in introducing progressive labor-management practices, such as employing nonwhite labor at high job and skill classification.[28]

Few American businesses have commented on this subject. Those that have stated that the investor does and must have social responsibility, since this will to a large extent determine the future of his investment, and that many American companies are striving to present a favorable image in a variety of ways, including "the attempt to deal with Africans on a humanized, individual basis rather than as an anonymous mass of men in a compound." They further state that, as in any part of the world, it is in the long-run interest of companies to provide training for better job opportunities, to offer individual advances based on ability, and to reduce turnover by providing satisfactory conditions of life and work for all employees.

[26] Philip W. Quigg, *South Africa: Problems and Prospects* (New York, The Council on Religion and International Affairs, 1965), p. 17, footnote 4.
[27] *United States–South African Relations,* Part I, p. 8.
[28] *Ibid.,* p. 46.

It seems reasonable to conclude that some American businesses are following enlightened policies and that others are not, but that the evidence is entirely too meager to base any even vaguely quantitative assessments. Even those companies with the most commendable records might be reluctant to supply the necessary data for the study required, if they were seen to be in conflict with job reservation and other restrictive legislation. It might also be held that concentration upon the conduct of American business, no matter how much one might wish it to be exemplary, is not the correct focus, that it is more pertinent to know whether economic growth in general is or is not contributing to improved conditions for the non-white in South Africa and to the eventual abandonment of apartheid.

IV: THE IMPACT OF AN IMPROVING ECONOMY

Many of the arguments for and against economic disengagement refer to the expected impact that such a policy would have on the economy of South Africa and the resultant expected impact on its political stance. Regrettably, the arguments are rarely pursued rigorously; some that are employed by each side are contradictory, and, occasionally, assumptions are also given as conclusions.

Numerous factors compound the difficulty of an objective assessment, including the paucity of available data and the lack of sufficient historical analogies to serve as guides to possible or likely courses of action. Other difficulties arise from the need to distinguish between economic and political forces and factors, between short- and long-run forces and expectations, and between economic injustice and inheritance of inferior circumstances or status.[29]

The purpose of this section is to examine whether or not the growing economy in South Africa is improving the material well-being of the African, and whether or not it is working against apartheid.

Those who favor economic disengagement usually argue that economic growth has not led to improvement in the political

[29] See William H. Hutt, *The Economics of the Colour Bar* (London, Andre Deutsch, 1964), in which economic injustice is defined as "any policy or action intended to perpetuate the inferiority of material standards or status of any racial group."

sphere, despite claims made over a century that it would. Some observers state or imply that bolstering the economy perpetuates
apartheid, which is different from noting that economic growth has
been accompanied or paralleled by political deprivation, since it
suggests a causal relationship. Others take the position that economic change does not support apartheid but that there is not
enough time for economic forces to achieve any satisfactory
change, or that these forces are not sufficiently powerful to do so.
Professor Karis, although noting that "the color-blind implications
of industrialization have conflicted with white attitudes of superi-
ority, self-interest and fear," [30] opines that "uninterrupted economic development undoubtedly will strengthen the present regime
in the short run by enlarging self-sufficiency and defensive strength
against both internal and external challenges." [31] Some observers
see economic forces as being essentially salubrious if given a
chance. Quigg, for example, notes "the inherent contradictions between economic integration and political and social segregation, between the liberating forces of the economic boom and the restrictive forces of political domination," but opines that economic prosperity, while "effecting small changes in the right direction . . .
holds out very limited promise." [32] Hutt's position is that "the fundamental injustice suffered by the Africans originates in those
hindrances to private investment which have condemned them as
a whole to avoidable backwardness," and that free enterprise has
worked wholly for the material advance of the non-white.[33]

There is, then, wide disagreement regarding the directional
thrust and strength of economic forces. Some interpretations appear
to be based upon the unsupported conclusion that, because a
booming economy has coincided with political oppression, there is
a cause-and-effect relationship. There are also certain questions
which probably should be, but which rarely are, asked, such as:
would oppression be less severe if the economy were retarded? how
would a retarded economy contribute to a desirable solution? and
would there be a greater propensity for political change under a

[30] Thomas Karis, *South Africa: The End Is Not Yet* (New York, Foreign Policy Association, Headline Series No. 176, April, 1966), p. 10.
[31] *Ibid.*, p. 40.
[32] Quigg, *South Africa*, p. 15.
[33] Hutt, *Economics of the Colour Bar*, p. 22.

depressed or a prosperous economy? In summary, the varying positions regarding the impact of economic advance include a surprising array of partially or wholly contradictory interpretations; it is seen by various observers as having no bearing, having an inadequate impact, having a beneficial impact only on material standards, comprising the means to a resolution of the problem if the South African government were rationally disposed, delaying the desired change, and expediting the desired change.

A wide range of studies would be required to shed light on this issue and hopefully to narrow the range of differences. Contributions from a variety of disciplines would be helpful, including attitudinal studies, demographic analyses, a search for historical analogies, and a variety of economic diagnoses. In the remainder of this paper a number of elements of the economic and demographic scene within South Africa are briefly examined, with the intention of assessing the strength of economic and demographic forces to impede or offset the stated goals of apartheid. This system comprises and is bolstered by a frightening array of repressive laws and edicts; it seeks to segregate the four major racial groups by a massive engineering of the urban, rural, and reserve landscapes; and above all it seeks to maintain in perpetuity the dominance of the whites in a country in which they comprise 19.0 percent of the population.

The General Impact of an Improving Economy

The broad claims for an improving economy are that it provides a stronger base for the future of all of the inhabitants of South Africa by broadening, diversifying, and modernizing the economy, that prosperity encourages wants and forces a share of power among rising social and racial groups. It is further argued that the objective of securing the economic, cultural, and social development of all races can best be achieved if the standards already achieved by the whites are being improved, an objective which "can be attained only by co-operation between the races in all spheres of the national life," [34] and which can best be achieved in

[34] H. F. Oppenheimer, "Towards Racial Harmony," supplement to *Optima* (September, 1956), unpaginated.

a strengthening economy. In the long run, then, an improving economy is seen as increasing the likelihood of change in political and racial theories and policies.

The validity of some of these claims cannot now be demonstrated in the case of South Africa. The evidence from a number of other countries suggests, however, that they cannot be dismissed out of hand. It seems reasonably obvious, for example, that economic prosperity has contributed greatly to the strengthened social, political, and economic position of the Negro population of the United States.

A second example is Spain. Partly through isolationism under Franco and partly through ostracism by Western Europe, this country was essentially removed from contact with modern economic forces from the Civil War to the mid-fifties. Since then several large infusions of capital, a remarkable tourist boom, and migration of Spaniards to employment in various Western European countries have ventilated the Spanish economy and polity, brought that country increasingly into the orbit of modern economic, political, and ethical forces, forced the abandonment or reduction of various restrictive policies, and strengthened the forces opposing the retrogressive policies of the dictatorship.

A third example is the negative case of Mozambique. If Portugal had paid greater attention to developing this territory, even if this had involved a greater dispersion of exploitation than already exists, the productive capacity of the country would have been increased, there would be a better infrastructure, Africans would be more involved in the money economy and less dependent upon migration to Rhodesia and South Africa, and, most important, there would be a lot more to take over when independence is achieved.

Impact on the Material Well-being of the African

If economic forces are in fact having a favorable impact in face of policies designed to restrict the role of the African in the modern economy, one would expect to see increasing percentages of Africans employed in certain sectors of the economy and wages improving more rapidly than average wages for the country. Unfortunately, data are not adequate to present as thorough an analysis of these subjects as would be desirable. But some concept of the trends may be obtained from the published statistics.

Employment. Current figures of employment are available for mining, manufacturing, construction, and transportation and communication combined for whites and for non-whites as a group. They indicate that the non-whites have made a very substantial gain in the numbers employed and a slight improvement in their share of employment in these combined sectors over the period 1954–55 to 1965–66 (Table 2). An index of employment is avail-

TABLE 2

South Africa: Employment in Mining,
Manufacturing, Construction, Transportation
and Communication, Selected Years,
1954–1966

		Whites		Non-whites	
	Total	*Number*		*Number*	
Year	*(in thousands)*	*(in thousands)*	*Percent*	*(in thousands)*	*Percent*
1954–55	1,518	395	26.0	1,123	74.0
1964–65	1,998	482	24.1	1,516	75.9
1965–56	2,058	497	24.1	1,561	75.9

SOURCES: Republic of South Africa, *Monthly Bulletin of Statistics*, Vol. XLV, No. 12 (December, 1966); *Bulletin of Statistics*, Vol. I, No. 1 (quarter ending June, 1967).

able for certain sectors, limited to the totals for all races and for whites (Table 3). For the sectors shown, whites have had the same increase in employment as the total increase only in transportation and communications; the greatest gains in employment by non-whites have been made in manufacturing and construction; the greatest relative gains of non-whites as compared with whites occurred in mining.

Data for some sectors do give the number of Africans employed; these are presented in Table 4, which shows the percentage share of African employment for selected years from 1957 to 1966 in mining, private manufacturing, and construction, and in Table 5, which, with the base year 1960, gives the indices of African em-

TABLE 3

South Africa: Index of Employment, Selected Years to 1965–1966

1953–1954 = 100

Year	Total		Mining		Manufacturing		Construction		Transportation and communication	
	All races	Whites	All races	Whites	All races	Whites	All races	Whites	All races	Whites
1954–55	103.9	101.3	103.3	104.1	104.7	101.3	104.7	102.1	102.6	100.0
1956–57	111.9	111.3	108.3	107.8	114.2 [a]	115.9 [a]	110.2 [a]	104.0 [a]	114.9	108.1
1958–59	112.9	112.7	112.8	105.2	114.3	118.6	101.4	97.8	114.8	111.1
1960–61	114.7	106.3	121.3	110.5	111.1	103.9	115.6	99.7	108.7	108.3
1962–63	122.5	114.8	120.7	108.7	128.5	121.0	125.2	109.3	110.4	111.1
1964–65	136.9	123.8	120.0	107.3	156.7	138.5	160.1	125.9	113.4	111.9
1965–66	141.0	127.6	122.8	107.3	160.1	142.7	180.0	142.1	114.7	114.2

SOURCE: Same as Table 2.

[a] Calendar year 1957.

TABLE 4

South Africa: Total Employment and Employment of Africans
in Mining, Private Manufacturing, and Construction,
Selected Years, 1957–1966

Year	Mining Total (in thousands)	Mining Percent of Bantu	Private Manufacturing Total (in thousands)	Private Manufacturing Percent of Bantu	Construction Total (in thousands)	Construction Percent of Bantu
1957	549	87.6	690	52.9	113	63.7
1960	593	88.4	692	51.7	104	68.2
1962–63	603	88.4	760	52.4	142	62.4
1965	607	88.6	930	53.2	182	67.0
1966	612	88.7	966[a]	52.3[a]	225[a]	67.9[a]

SOURCE: Same as Table 2.
[a] 10-month average.

TABLE 5

South Africa: Indices of Population Growth and Employment
of Africans in Specific Sectors, 1965, 1966 (partial)
1960 = 100

	1965	1966
Population (estimated)	112.0	114.5
Employment		
Mining	102.6	103.5
Manufacturing	137.9	141.2[a]
Construction	174.3	215.5[a]
Railways and Harbors	101.1	98.7[b]
Post Office	163.5	165.2[b]
Central Government	116.0	212.2[c]
Provincial Administration [c]	133.3	143.5[c]
Local Authorities	109.0	115.9[c]
Total, above categories	118.0	123.2[e]

SOURCE: Same as Table 2.
[a] 10 months.
[b] June, 1966.
[c] January–February, 1966.
[d] Base year 1961.
[e] Estimate.

ployment in a number of employment categories as compared with the index of estimated population growth. Table 5, which included 1,336,600 African employees in 1960, 1,576,900 in 1965, and an estimated 1,646,200 in 1966 (partial), reveals that employment of Africans grew more rapidly than population in all categories shown except mining and the South African Railways and Harbours, the latter having long been used as a kind of white preserve. Total employment in the categories listed increased from 1960 to 1966 (partial) at a rate 1.6 times the estimated rate of population growth.

The trends in employment are, then, generally favorable. That there has been a marked improvement in more recent years is indicated by an average annual increase of 45,333 jobs for Africans in private manufacturing and 16,000 in construction in the period 1962–65, or at a rate almost double the average for 1960–65. It has been estimated that the number of non-whites in actual employment is now increasing at a rate 1.69 times the increase in the economically active non-white population. In face of the increasing body of apartheid legislation these figures would suggest that economic forces are having a not inconsiderable countereffect.

Wages. Data regarding salaries and wages are even less adequate than for numbers employed. No over-all estimates are given and recent figures are not available for several important sectors, particularly agriculture. Some occupations provide food, accommodations, and free medical facilities which may be valued at anywhere from one fifth to one half of wages.

The record with respect to wages was a deplorable one from the prewar years to the late 1950s. D. Hobart Houghton has estimated that in 1935 the ratio of white to non-white wages in mining was 11:1 while in 1960 it was almost 16½ :1.[35] H. Goldberg has shown that African wages in manufacturing increased from 1946 to 1958 less rapidly than the cost of living, resulting in a 4 percent decline

[35] D. Hobart Houghton, *The South African Economy* (Cape Town, Oxford University Press, 1964), p. 161. See also W. F. J. Steenkamp, "The Bantu Wage Problem," *South African Journal of Economics*, June, 1962, and J. A. Lombard, *The Determination of Racial Income Differentials in South Africa* (Durban, University of Natal Institute for Social Research, 1962).

in purchasing power in the twelve-year period.[36] Hutt also calculated that the average annual earnings of non-whites in private
manufacturing had declined from 24.6 percent of white earnings in
1925–26 to 20.6 percent in 1958–59.[37]

More recent years have witnessed some improvement in this generally dismal record. Not in mining, however, where average white
wages in 1964–65 were still 16.9 times the average African wage, a
ratio that has changed only imperceptibly since 1960. The explanations for this persistently poor record, according to Houghton, include the insulation of African wages from the operation of supply
and demand due to the monopsonist position of the Chamber of
Mines, government restrictions on the use of labor, and the predominance of foreign Africans in this industry. The gold mining industry, which employs about 64 percent of all African miners,
maintains that the fixed price of gold prohibits keeping pace with
the rise in wages in other sectors, and that provision of food and
lodging permits the contract worker to save a larger share of his
earnings than is possible in other occupations. They also note that
workers apply voluntarily in adequate numbers, particularly from
Lesotho, Botswana, Mozambique, and Malawi where average
wages are lower than on the mines and adequate job opportunities
are not available.[38] Certain mines in South Africa and South West
Africa are reported to have raised wages sharply in the last few
years, but the total record in this industry still leaves a great deal to
be desired.

The current trend with respect to wages in manufacturing is considerably more satisfactory (Table 6). From 1960 to the first half of
1966 average wages increased by 45.3 percent while the cost of liv-

[36] H. Goldberg, *Work Opportunities, Labour Utilisation: A Function of Management* (Johannesburg, Bantu Wage and Productivity Association, 1965), p. 6.
[37] Hutt, *Economics of the Colour Bar*, p. 181.
[38] In 1965 there were an estimated 650,000 foreign Africans working in South
Africa. Most were contract laborers on the mines and farms, but a considerable
number have been resident in the Republic long enough so that they really
have no other home. In the long run there is an advantage to South Africa in
the high percentage of foreign Africans employed in gold mining. Employment
in this sector is decreasing and a peak production is expected in from five to
ten years after which employment will probably decline more sharply as successive mines reach the end of their lives. The impact of such a decline on
Africans from the Republic will thus be minimized. The impact on the source
countries, particularly Lesotho, could, however, be very serious.

TABLE 6

South Africa: Employment and Wages of Africans
in Mining and Private Manufacturing,
Selected Years, 1957–1966 [a]

		Mining [b]		
	Number	Average annual per capita wage		
Year	employed (in thousands)	$ equivalent	Real $ wage [c]	Percent of average wage for all races
1957	481	$183.3	$189.3	36.1
1960	524	197.7	191.9	37.0
1965	538	241.9 [d]	216.0 [d]	37.3 [d]
1966 [a]	547	250.0	212.0	36.7

		Private manufacturing		
	Number	Average annual per capita wage		
Year	employed (in thousands)	$ equivalent	Real $ wage [c]	Percent of average wage for all races
1957	365	$433.3	$447.6	41.5
1960	358	484.8	470.7	41.5
1965	495	622.2 [d]	541.5 [d]	46.0 [d]
1966 [a]	505	704.3	597.0	45.4

SOURCE: Same as Table 2.
[a] First half 1966 at annual rate.
[b] Employees also receive food, lodging, and medical services as part of their remuneration.
[c] 1958 = 100.
[d] 1964–65.

ing rose by 14.6 percent. In the latter year the average annual wage of Africans in manufacturing was $704. Wages also rose more rapidly than the average for all employees in manufacturing, increasing from 41.5 percent of the average for all races in 1960 to 45.4 percent in 1966. The Bantu Wage and Productivity Association has shown that neither the increase in numbers employed nor the rise in per capita wages has had an inflationary effect on the industrial cost structure, thus countering a favorite argument of those who would prefer to see wage increases more rigidly controlled.[39]

[39] See H. Goldberg, "Productivity," in *Productivity, Responsibility and Development* (Johannesburg, Bantu Wage and Productivity Association, 1966), pp. 4–5.

Increased Skills and Training. An improving economy should result in gains for all racial groups in increased skills, training, and knowledge of modern economic processes. Here the data available are completely inadequate to formulate an accurate concept of the changing status for the non-white in South Africa. The censuses of 1946 and 1960 indicated that there had been an increase from 27,148 to 54,203 in Africans classified as professional, technical, administrative, and related workers; in 1960 this represented 1.4 percent of total economically engaged Africans as compared to 17.1 percent for whites in these same categories. Disparities cannot, of course, be taken as *ipso facto* evidence of discrimination since they reflect in part the relative scarcity of skilled manpower in a predominantly less advanced population group.

Nonetheless, a complex of written and unwritten impediments obviously places entirely indefensible and uneconomic blocks to African advance. The pressure against various job reservation prescriptions is briefly discussed in a later section. The educational impediments in South Africa are also to be deplored,[40] whether or not the numbers being educated and trained compare favorably with most African countries. One favorable sign is the tentative permission of the government to permit non-white engineering students to enroll at Cape Town and Witwatersrand universities. Without a much more detailed analysis, about all that can be concluded is that Africans are making gains in the acquisition of skills, training, and familiarity with the modern economy, but that a mass of restrictions limit their advance so that their participation in and contribution to the economy are much lower than they should or could be.

Consumption Power. The consumption power of Africans should, of course, be enlarged by an improving economy. Again measures are not adequate to provide much of a clue to the over-all rate of improvement. Difficulties include the sparseness of statistical series, the inadequacy of data from the reserves, and the problem of measuring payments in kind.

[40] See UNESCO, *The Effects of "Apartheid" on Education, Science, Culture and Information in South Africa.* Draft, January 18, 1967 (in press).

Estimates of African incomes and of total African consumption power vary substantially. Two studies estimated the per capita incomes by racial group for 1960 as shown in Table 7.

TABLE 7

South Africa: Estimated Per Capita Incomes by
Racial Groups, 1960

	E.E.C.[a]	Bak [b]
Whites	$1,148	$1,333
Coloured	224	206
Asians	162	153
Africans	129	122

[a] E.E.C., *Government Expenditures and Racial Discrimination* (E/CN.14/189), January 24, 1963.

[b] C. Bak, University of South Africa (dissertation), 1964.

N.B. The following calculations must be taken as extremely crude and as showing only very rough orders of magnitude. If one takes the figure of $125 as the average per capita income of Africans in South Africa in 1960, and if one assumes that the African share of national income increased proportionately to the increase in national income, then the estimated per capita income of Africans would have been $174 in 1964. This would compare with estimated average incomes for tropical Africa as a whole of about $100–115 and with per capita incomes for specific countries as follows: Gabon, $333 (1963); Ivory Coast, $188 (1964); Sierra Leone, $125 (1964); and Tanzania, $63 (1964). These are the only countries for which national income figures are given by the International Monetary Fund. Note that both the income figures above and the per capita gross domestic product figures below apply only to Africans in South Africa but to all races for other countries.

If one further assumes that the per capita share of the gross domestic product of Africans in South Africa has the same ratio to the g.d.p. that their per capita income has to the total national income, then the per capita share of the g.d.p. of Africans in South Africa would have been $206 in 1964. This would compare with per capita share of the g.d.p. of tropical African countries in 1964 as follows:

Malawi	$30	(1963)	Togo	$ 97		Rhodesia	$240
Nigeria	58	(1963)	Sudan	108	(1963)	Ivory Coast	244
Tanzania	59		Sierra Leone	146		Ghana	246
Uganda	66		Zambia	177		Liberia	269
Kenya	86		Senegal	198		Gabon	418

Above estimates derived from U.N. *Monthly Bulletin of Statistics* (November, 1966), and International Monetary Fund, *International Financial Statistics* (April, 1967).

Estimates of total African income include those shown in Table 8. The distribution of African income by geographical area has also

TABLE 8

Estimated Total Incomes of Africans in South Africa

Source	Year	Estimate (in million $)	Estimated percentage share of total	Remarks
a	1961	$1,378	23	Cash income estimated at $1,003 million.
b	1963	1,680		Cash income estimated at $1,400 million.
c	1963	1,050		
d	1965	1,680	20	
e	1965	1,400		
f	1966	1,680		

SOURCES:
a. H. J. J. Reynders, *Bantu,* March, 1965, quoted in South African Institute of Race Relations, *A Survey of Race Relations in South Africa, 1965,* p. 204.
b. C. DeConing, "The Bantu Consumer in a Plural Society," in *Planning for the Bantu Market* (National Development and Management Foundation of South Africa, 1966).
c. G. M. Leistner, "Economic and Demographic Aspects of the Bantu Market," *ibid.*
d. *Natal Mercury,* February 16, 1965, as quoted in *A Survey . . . 1965,* pp. 204–5.
e. *Bantu,* February, 1965, as quoted *ibid.,* p. 205.
f. Republic of South Africa, *South African Scope,* January, 1967, p. 7.

been the subject of varying estimates. DeConing estimated that the one quarter of Africans living in urban areas accounted for half the total. Leistner estimated that Africans in urban areas received 60 percent of the total; those in white rural areas, 31 percent; and those in the reserves, 9 percent. The Bantu Investment Corporation estimated that urban Africans commanded 50 percent of total purchasing power; those in the reserves, 28 percent; and those on white-owned farms, 22 percent.[41] The relatively high percent of the total earned by urban Africans suggests that it is important to measure the influx of Africans to the cities and to attempt to determine the power of economic forces in sustaining this influx in face of government policies to reduce it; this subject is briefly examined in a later section.

[41] South African Institute of Race Relations, *A Survey of Race Relations in South Africa, 1965,* p. 204.

Whatever the average or total incomes may be, there is increasing evidence that many Africans are living below the poverty datum line. The Bantu Wage and Productivity Association estimated that 45 percent of workers in 1965 were receiving wages below a poverty datum line of $67 per month and that starting wages were far below this line. Sheila Suttner concluded that many families in Soweto, a huge African township based on Johannesburg, were not receiving the minimum requirements, which were placed at $78 per month in 1966.[42] Numerous other studies have shown comparable results.[43] And the validity of the poverty datum line has also been questioned, since budgets based on this line do not include expenditures for furniture and household goods, repairs, medicines and toilet requisites, tobacco, school fees and books, reading matter, insurance, or recreation. An alternative and more realistic level would be the "effective minimum income," which would be about half again as high as the poverty datum line.[44]

As has been seen, wages in manufacturing are now rising more rapidly than the cost of living, but they are probably not keeping pace with the mounting needs of the increasingly westernized Africans in several other sectors. The growing number of budget and cost-of-living studies have made a very significant contribution in revealing the scope of the problem. They have strengthened the pleas for higher wages which have been made by an increasing number of industrialists, associations, and other organizations.

Economic and Demographic Integration in South Africa

The next subject for examination is the impact of economic forces on economic integration in South Africa. Since demographic factors have force in their own right and are closely associated with economic integration, they must also be included in this brief as-

[42] Sheila Suttner, "Cost of Living in Soweto," South African Institute of Race Relations, 1966.
[43] Including studies by Rhodes University, the Bureau of Market Research of the University of South Africa, the University of Natal, the University of Stellenbosch, and the Institute of Race Relations.
[44] A Survey . . . 1965, pp. 205–6.

sessment. The thesis to be analyzed is that economic forces associated with an expanding economy lead to increasing economic integration of racial groups, which is the opposite of what is intended by apartheid. Pressures against apartheid are seen in an increasing urbanization and geographic integration, in moves to offset influx control and job reservation, and in the increased dependence of the economy on the African market.

Increased Urbanization and Integration. Table 9 shows for four

TABLE 9

The Urban Population of South Africa

Year	Total urban population (in thousands)	Percent of total population of each group				
		All races	Whites	African	Coloured	Asian
1936	3,204	33.4	67.9	18.9	57.2	71.4
1946	4,393	38.5	74.6	23.7	60.9	71.2
1951	5,397	42.6	78.4	27.2	64.6	77.4
1960	7,475	46.8	83.7	31.7	69.0	83.0

Year	Percent of total urban population by racial group			
	Whites	African	Coloured	Asian
1936	42.5	38.8	13.7	5.0
1946	40.3	42.3	12.8	4.6
1951	38.4	43.2	13.2	5.2
1960	34.6	46.2	13.9	5.3

SOURCE: Same as Table 2.

census years the percent of the total population of each racial group in urban areas, and the percent of the total urban population by racial group. As may be seen, there has been a steady increase in the percent of urbanized Africans and a growing predominance of non-whites over whites in these communities. Data are not available after 1960, but the indices of employment (Table 5) suggest that there has probably been little if any slackening in the rate of growth of the urban African population despite influx control. Evidence of this is seen in the estimate that between 1962 and 1965 the African population of Johannesburg increased from 609,100 to 713,808.

The African population is now distributed approximately as follows: urban areas, 35 percent; rural white areas, 30 percent; and reserves, 35 percent. The proportion of Africans to the total population has increased over the past decades both in the cities and in the white rural areas, where they have more than replaced the decline in white population.[45] Indeed the only places where the proportion of Africans to the total population has shrunk are those areas where they had constituted over 90 percent of the population in 1911.[46]

It will be increasingly difficult to measure the urban-white rural-reserve distribution of the African population because of the growing tendency for Africans working in certain cities or in border industrial areas to be housed in a "reserve" fairly close at hand. Many reserve townships would, however, be just as much a part of the urban agglomeration as the townships in the white areas.

Looking to the future, the composition of the population in the year 2000 might be approximately as follows: whites, 6.15 million; Africans, 28.0 million; Coloureds, 4.7 million; and Asians, 1.25 million.[47] If these figures are used, it would mean that the percent of the total population of each racial group would be as follows compared with the 1966 figures, given in parentheses: whites, 15.3 (19.0); Africans, 69.9 (68.1); Coloureds, 11.7 (9.9); and Asians, 3.1 (3.0). It may be noted that the combined Coloured and Asian population would nearly equal that of the whites, and, if one ac-

[45] T. J. D. Fair and N. Manfred Shaffer, "Population Patterns and Policies in South Africa," *Economic Geography* (July, 1964), pp. 261–74.
[46] Harold C. Brookfield, "Some Geographical Implications of the Apartheid and Partnership Policies in South Africa," *Institute of British Geographers Transactions and Papers* (No. 23, 1957), pp. 225–47.
[47] These estimates were calculated by the author on the basis of the white population having a slow decline in the natural rate of increase plus 20,000 net immigrants per year, the Asians and Coloureds having a somewhat more rapid decline in the rate of increase, and the Africans having a slow increase in this rate. The projected figure for the African population is well above the Tomlinson Commission's higher estimate of 21.4 million, not far above the estimates made by M. S. DuToit and L. T. Badenhorst, and slightly below the projection made by Dr. F. W. Fox of the South African Institute for Medical Research. See *A Survey . . . 1965*, p. 111.

cepts the Tomlinson Commission estimate that the maximum number of Africans who could be accommodated in the reserves by A.D. 2000 is 10 million, including 2 million migrant workers outside the reserves, it follows that the non-white population resident in white areas permanently or temporarily would be 2.6 times the white population as compared with the present ratio of about 2.3 to 1.

The policy of apartheid is quite obviously related to the population dynamics of South Africa. But demographic forces alone would appear to make it impossible of achievement. Government efforts to alter the population ratio have been focused upon the attraction of white immigrants to the country. The record is shown in Table 10.

TABLE 10

South Africa: White Migration,
Selected Periods, 1925–1929 to 1966

Year	Immigrants	Emigrants	Net gain or loss
1925–29	33,546	19,994	+13,552
1930–34	20,875	13,255	+ 7,620
1935–39	39,006	15,969	+23,037
1940–44	8,044	10,419	− 2,375
1945–49	92,835	38,520	+54,315
1950–54	80,192	61,356	+18,836
1955–59	63,057	54,522	+ 8,535
1960	9,789	12,612	− 2,823
1961	16,309	14,903	+ 1,406
1962	20,916	8,945	+11,971
1963	37,964	7,156	+30,808
1964	40,865	8,092	+32,773
1965	38,326	9,206	+29,120
1966	48,048	9,888	+38,160

SOURCES: Union of South Africa, Bureau of Census and Statistics, *Union Statistics for Fifty Years, 1910–1960;* Republic of South Africa, *Monthly Bulletin of Statistics,* various issues; *Bulletin of Statistics,* Vol. I, No. 1.

A continuation of the high level of net immigration of 1963–65 would not, however, alter the dominance of non-whites in the white area.[48] And even a large white immigration creates concern

[48] Space does not permit an assessment of the chances of sustaining a high level of immigration, which could be affected by a multitude of factors. It may

among some Afrikaners, for it reduces their fraction of the total and thus threatens their culture, religion, and the Afrikaner way of life. This has led to the suggestions that there be "selective breeding" to strengthen the Afrikaner strain and that white couples plan to increase the number of children they bear.

It seems clear, in summary, that the objective of separate development—decreasing the number of Africans in the white areas—is unlikely to be achieved. Predictions that the flow of Africans to white areas will be reversed by 1978 and that the year 2000 will see the African population there at the same level as it was in 1950 appear to be totally unrealistic. The government is attempting to move against two forces—economic and demographic—which are probably too powerful to be denied.

Influx Control and Job Reservation. Two of apartheid's most potent weapons are job reservation regulations and influx control. Job reservation laws were promulgated in the industrial Conciliation Acts of 1924, 1956, and 1959; determinations are issued irregularly and may reserve certain jobs for whites, set quotas for employment in specific jobs by race, and fix compulsory minimum ratios of white to non-white labor. Determinations may apply locally, regionally, or nationally. Influx control is provided by the Bantu Laws Amendment Act (No. 42 of 1964), which augmented, reinforced and codified eleven previous acts controlling the presence and employment of Africans in all parts of South Africa outside the reserves. Under this act all urban areas, most towns, and peri-urban areas are classified as "prescribed areas." To enter such an area an African must secure a permit from a labor bureau; any African may also be endorsed out of any prescribed area no matter how long he may have lived there.

In examining the question of whether economic forces are operating against these oppressive regulations, we may first look briefly at influx control. Much of the evidence presented in the sec-

---

be noted, however, that a substantial percent of recent migrants have come from Kenya, Rhodesia, and Zambia. A collapse of the Smith regime in Rhodesia could lead to a large-scale migration from that country, but the total European population of the countries north of the Limpopo is not adequate to maintain a high level of migration to the Republic for any lengthy period.

tion on employment indicates that it certainly has not succeeded in meeting officially stated goals, primarily because the burgeoning economy has required the admission of far more people than the number which could be endorsed out.

Even in the Western Cape, from which the government has decreed that all Africans are to be removed (and presumably replaced by Coloureds), the shortage of white and Coloured personnel has meant that an increasing number of Africans have had to be recruited. The whole scheme has, in fact, been opposed by many industrialists, farmers, and political leaders, primarily because of the growing need for workers. What influx control in this area has done is to make the African labor force more migratory and to widen the disparity in the male-female ratio. While Africans are supposed to return at their own expense to their "homelands" upon the expiration of a contract and to pay the round-trip fare if they are re-recruited, there appears to be a considerable amount of subterfuge by both management and labor to bypass these arbitrary restrictions.

There is substantial doubt that even the government really wants what it says it wants, which raises serious questions regarding its theoretical claims for apartheid. Officials have stated in practically the same breath that the flow of Africans to the Witwatersrand must be stopped, but that influx control would not be allowed to interfere with industrial development there. More and more, apartheid appears to be a cynical rationalization for maintaining the dominance of the white community. The goal is not that of separate development but of separate voting bases; thus the white can have just the amount of labor required in his areas while the African is expected to be satisfied by the promise of eventual political rights in an area in which he may have no interest whatsoever.

This is not to say that the partial failure of influx control has softened its impact on many Africans. The Black Sash wrote in 1966 in this regard:

For thousands of Africans these laws result in broken families, in unemployment, in poverty and malnutrition, insecurity and instability, and in a state of hopelessness. Millions of rands are spent . . . and millions of man-hours are wasted in the attempt to enforce unenforceable laws. The real cost must be counted in terms of human sorrow, bitterness, suffering, and tragedy on a vast scale.[49]

The government's proposed methods of halting the flow to the Witwatersrand and other areas are to seek dependence on a smaller labor force, to mechanize and automate, to decentralize industry, particularly in border areas, and to develop the so-called homelands. The first is not at all likely so long as the economy continues to expand; improving productivity may result in the loss of specific jobs but will more strongly enforce the economic boom and create other jobs; the ability of the border industry and reserve development programs to meet the stated goals is examined later.

Influx control enforces the migrant labor system, which is extremely inefficient and wasteful. This system precludes the employment of a substantial segment of the potential labor force and thus contributes to inflation by aggravating the labor shortage. It adds unnecessarily to the costs of transportation and training, results in lower productivity, fosters a careless management of African labor, and may force the employer to accept wholly unqualified labor.[50] The African, under the migratory system, is less able to acquire skills, has less incentive to do so, must often work for an employer, in a job, or at a place over none of which he has any control, and is subjected to disruption of his family and social life, all of which reduces his possible contribution to the economy. The more forward-looking employers are seeking to mitigate the effects of the migrant system through better selection processes, more effective training, reemployment of former workers, and a more humanized labor relations policy.

Job reservation, like influx control, is unsound economically, and various of the determinations have come under increasing pressure from the business community in South Africa. Economically, its most obvious disadvantage is that it creates artificial shortages of professional, skilled, and semiskilled personnel, which places an unnecessary brake on the country's growth and contributes to inflation. By placing a ceiling on advance of the non-whites it reduces

[49] *Memorandum on the Application of the Pass Laws and Influx Control,* quoted in South African Institute of Race Relations, *A Survey of Race Relations in South Africa, 1966,* pp. 168–69.
[50] Houghton, *South African Economy,* p. 87.

their incentive and hence their efficiency, while the reverse protection of the whites reduces their incentive and efficiency. Job reservation is economically wasteful also because its effect on incomes reduces the size of the domestic market.

The economic boom in South Africa has resulted in formidable shortages at all levels above the unskilled. It has also made many South Africans aware, perhaps for the first time, of the country's great potential and of the necessity to have non-whites integrated more fully into the economy. Government-proposed solutions to the problem are to increase white immigration, to raise productivity, to extend the working age of whites, and to train them for higher posts. None of these, nor all of them combined, are capable of meeting the needs.

An increasing number of South African business leaders are protesting against the restrictive labor regulations.[51] The Transvaal Chamber of Industries wrote in 1964 that "the most effective and satisfactory means of expanding . . . manpower resources would be to train semi-skilled workers regardless of race" and that "there is no doubt that employers are keen to develop the skills of Bantu workers." [52] There have also been strong objections to specific job reservation determinations on the part of several industries, including vehicle assembly, clothing, and textile firms, and the government has, in fact, been induced to grant numerous exemptions and to relax or waive others.[53]

What appears to be happening under the pressure of the shortage of semiskilled and skilled workers is that "employers have

[51] Organizations which have called for relaxation of restrictive labor regulations include the government's Economic Advisory Council, the National Federation of Building Trade Employees, the Industrial Economics Division of the Council for Scientific and Industrial Research, the National Institute for Personnel Research, the Chambers of Commerce of Cape Town, Johannesburg, and other cities, the Association of Chambers of Commerce, the South African Federated Chamber of Industries, and the Transvaal Chamber of Industries.

[52] Quoted in South African Institute of Race Relations, *A Survey of Race Relations in South Africa, 1964,* p. 241.

[53] Even the state-owned railways, which have long been a preserve for whites, and the white union, whose members were given a substantial wage increase at the time, agreed late in 1965 to permit African workers to perform certain skilled jobs. In the same year white miners forced the abandonment of an experiment, sanctioned both by the union and by the government, to allow Africans to perform certain skilled underground jobs, but in 1967 the experiment was again applied with government approval.

inched the colour bar higher and higher without hurt to anyone and without fanfare and fuss." [54] By January, 1965, according to the Deputy Minister of Labour, some 39 percent of active Africans were being employed as operatives or as semiskilled workers.

Various techniques are employed in efforts to meet the existing labor shortages. At one end of the scale, white skills are spread more thinly by job fragmentation and work subdivisions; since whites can thus be given higher wages they raise few if any objections to having non-whites move up below them. At the other end, restrictions are being breached or broken, with non-whites doing white-only jobs more and more openly in both private and public employment, and many Africans being employed in place of non-existent white operatives at full operatives' wages.

Employers and organizations are also devoting more attention to the training of non-white workers, while their promotion to more skilled jobs provides experience for further upgrading. The National Development and Management Foundation, for example, has a training scheme for non-white supervisors, with an increasing number of African men, previously known as "boss-boys," being given instruction in personnel relations, welfare and clerical work. And, as noted earlier, the Department of Bantu Administration agreed in principle and as a temporary measure to the Straszacker Commission recommendation that Africans be admitted to engineering courses at two universities.

Needless to say, the record still leaves a great deal to be desired and progress cannot be expected to be sustained without friction. Traditional fears may still override the need for more efficient use of manpower. And the government may be expected to react to what it sees as a threatening trend. The Deputy Minister of Bantu Administration and Development, for example, stated in April, 1965, that Africans would not be able to develop economically above a certain level and that, while the bar was elastic, it would not be moved all the way to the top.[55]

Increasing Dependence on the African Market. One of the less publicized influences of the growing economic integration of Afri-

[54] Editorial in *The Star* (Johannesburg), November 14, 1964.
[55] *A Survey . . . 1965*, p. 2.

can workers is the increasing significance of the African market to the entire economy. South Africans have not, in general, seen that rising employment and, particularly, rising wages have a strongly generative and multiplying effect, though a greater acceptance of these connections is beginning to develop. As this understanding grows there should result an increased desire to reduce the jobless and the numbers of Africans still in the subsistence sector, which will be increasingly seen as a serious drag on the economy.

The manufacturing sector, in particular, must be greatly concerned to extend its markets. And it is essential to the economic health of the country that it do so, since the gold industry will reach its peak production in the fairly near future. South Africa should also look to enlarged markets in the rest of Africa, but it cannot expect to become the workshop of the continent unless it adopts more acceptable racial policies.

Inability of the Reserves to Meet the Needs. Two of the government programs designed to justify apartheid are the development of the reserves and the promotion of border industries. These must be briefly examined to determine the possibility of their success and their ability to offset the integration which they are intended to reduce.

The reserves and Bantustans cannot be expected to fill the bill for a multitude of reasons. Politically the reserves are so fragmented (c. 238 separate blocks) as to be unsuitable for nationhood, while the projected consolidation appears to be almost incapable of achievement.[56] The identification of Chiefs with the government also tends to drive a wedge between them and their people, which is the exact opposite of the government's professed intentions. Potential dangers for the future include the expectation that the urbanized African will not be interested in or satisfied with casting his vote in a "homeland" which he may never have known or which is increasingly foreign to him; the likelihood of unrest if the Chiefs or local governments were coerced; the repercussions that might result if emergency powers were applied to a supposedly self-

[56] If the number of separate blocks is reduced at the same rate as it was from 1954 to 1963 it would require about 70 years to consolidate them into nine Bantustans.

governing area; and the difficulty if not impossibility of retaining forever a long list of reserve powers in what are proposed as states with equal rights.

Demographically, the reserves are already overpopulated. With an area of roughly 58,014 square miles (including the Transkei), their population density is about 75 per square mile compared to about 34 per square mile in the remainder of the Republic. Their agricultural resources are entirely inadequate to sustain the present population even under the scientifically most rational land use methods. The reserves are characteristically overworked, over-grazed, and more or less damaged by erosion. Almost none are self-sufficient in food production, several of the larger reserves depending on white farms for at least 25–40 percent of their food supply. In those areas which have been "planned," the government has found it impossible to remove all of the surplus families from the land, which has led to the splitting of units and the perpetuation of uneconomic holdings. Irrespective of whether separate development is acceptable or workable, the rationalization of reserve areas should be extended, since it represents a net gain to the African and to the productive capacity of the country. But the land alone cannot support the numbers that the government expects to live permanently in the reserves, since at least 1½ million people should be taken off the land.

The opportunities for other employment are also entirely inadequate at the present time. In 1966, for example, only 33,007 Africans were in paid employment in the Transkei, which has received the greatest attention. This number compares with an estimated 258,000 employed outside the territory, including 118,000 long-term if not permanent migrants. There are possibilities for development of mining, forestry, and other activities in a number of the reserves, but they do not add up to the creation of enough jobs even to approach the need.

The only possible answer to supporting the present population or an expanded population in the reserves would appear to be a large-scale development of manufacturing. But here the government places severe restrictions on the prospect by prohibiting capital investment not approved by the Bantu Investment Corporation or the Xhosa Development Corporation, whose resources are inadequate. The prospects are further inhibited by the shortage of available skills, the lack of resources, and the small size of the reserve markets. At present the Transkei has only a handful of factories worthy of the name and these employ fewer than 500 Africans.

Another reason why the reserve program is inadequate is that the government is not allocating sufficient funds to it. Expenditures have increased from $12.1 million in 1956–61 to about $59 million in 1965–66, but about one quarter of the latter was expended for land purchase. The amount available for appropriation from all sources in the Transkei increased from $18 million in 1961–62 to $26 million in 1966–67. Defense expenditures in the 1966–67 South African budget totaled $360 million by comparison, and only about 5.5 percent of investment in public projects is allocated to the African areas.

Finally, the concept of "homelands" and reserve development is no policy at all with respect to the Coloured and Asian groups.

The facts that Lesotho and Botswana are now independent countries (with the former being entirely surrounded by the Republic and adjacent to the Transkei) and that they are economically comparable to the South African reserves may affect the evolution of policy with respect to the latter. The governments of these two countries, both of which are heavily dependent upon their economic relations with South Africa, have adopted policies calling for continued friendly relations with the Republic. Swaziland is expected to do the same when it becomes independent, probably as Ngwane.

Allistair Sparks, foreign editor of the *Rand Daily Mail,* believes that "the business of having to maintain decent relations with independent Black states, of having to meet and deal with their leaders, can in time bring about some adjustments in thinking and attitude," most importantly by lowering the level of racial fear, and that it will "hopefully bring about a greater sympathy and understanding of Black Africa" on the part of South African whites.[57]

[57] Allistair Sparks "Lesotho, Botswana, Swaziland: The Implications of Independence," South African Institute of Race Relations, 1967, reproduced as "A Time for Detente?—South Africa: A View from Within," *Africa Report,* March, 1967, pp. 40–45.

In the context of the reserve program, the examples of Lesotho, Botswana, and Swaziland may have a significant impact on certain economic policies. If white South African capital can go to Lesotho, for example, what is the justification for restricting its flow to the Transkei? If a friendly and independent Lesotho decided to have freehold tenure, why should this not be permitted in the Transkei, if the Bantustan government so desires? A few voices have already been raised in favor of permitting "white" capital initiative to speed the development of the Transkei and even of allowing mixed international support for such development. It is not impossible that the government would accede to such steps, although it has stated that they would never be allowed on the basis of granting permanent rights to the whites in the African areas.

Border Industries as a Possible Alternative. The border industry program of the South African government is designed to reduce the number of Africans permanently or semipermanently residing in white areas, by providing employment for workers who would presumably commute daily from the reserves to factories on the white side of the border. If it is accepted, as proposed above, that the only way in which adequate employment opportunities could be created to support a larger reserve population is through promotion of manufacturing, it follows that border industries could conceivably meet this need. Hence their potential contribution must be examined.

The accomplishments of the program to date have not been particularly impressive. In the period from 1960 to mid-1965 it is claimed that $252 million were invested in border industries, that aid was extended to 88 new industrial establishments and for 57 expansions of existing plants, while 52 new concerns went unaided to border areas. In mid-1965 all industries in and near the borders were employing an estimated 95,000 Africans. New border industries provided for only about 8,250 persons a year from 1960 to 1966, whereas, if border industries were to stop the flow of Africans to the cities, 34,800 new border jobs a year would be required, according to the Deputy Minister of Bantu Administration and Development. This would require the establishment of more new industries on the borders of the reserves than in the remainder of the white areas.

The border industrial program contains advantages and disadvantages for both the Africans and the whites. Advantages for the Africans include the following: certain influx control and color-bar regulations do not apply to border industries; families would be less likely to be separated; heads of families can own land in freehold in a reserve township, can own or rent a house, and can build a house at lower cost; more money will be brought home and will be spent in the reserves in enterprises owned by Africans; the townships might be expected to stimulate production of market produce in the reserves; and the resident of a reserve township would be subjected to less onerous regulations respecting his activities.

On the other hand, the African would be on a lower wage scale, would work longer hours, and would have less paid leave; the ceiling on his advance would still apply; it would be more difficult to establish competing industries in the reserves; and the program, while being completely inadequate to meet the needs, would provide a convenient rationalization for the whites. Furthermore, not all of the advantages of the reserve townships would be realized. Tenure is insecure, since rights may be canceled if a tenant ceases in the manager's opinion to be a "fit and proper" person to live in the township; [58] some residents would be further away from the place of employment than in a municipal township, thus raising the cost of transportation and the expenditure of time in commuting; and not all families of workers would be united since this would require relinquishment of land holdings which might be situated deep in the reserve.

An advantage of border industries to the government is that it is cheaper to build houses in the reserves, where wages are lower and productivity of construction workers is not circumscribed by union regulations. Over half of development plan expenditures for the reserves has thus far gone to housing, primarily for border townships within the reserves, about 24,000 dwellings having been constructed in 35 townships in the reserves by March, 1966.

[58] See *A Survey . . . 1965*, pp. 191–94.

Advantages to the white employer include provision of a variety of incentives extended by the government;[59] a lower wage scale; the assurance of a plentiful and possibly a more permanent labor supply; and the fact that he need not provide housing, recreational or hospital facilities.

The disadvantages of the border industry program to the white community in general are that it would have an unfavorable impact on the market, whose disintegration they might later come to regret; that it may provide unfair competition to existing industry and undermine the whole system of collective bargaining;[60] and that there are costs associated with the uneconomic location of industries. Furthermore, there are serious doubts that the security of whites, which the program is said to provide, would in fact be improved. And lastly, the program does not lead to separation but rather to economic integration, as the Tomlinson Commission concluded in its lukewarm projection of the concept. The essential difference from present conditions is that whites would migrate permanently to the borders of African areas instead of Africans migrating to white urban areas.

It must be noted that some existing urban centers are situated sufficiently close to reserves that they could be considered to be border areas. This is true particularly for Pretoria, the Durban-Pietermaritzburg axis, East London, and Pietersburg. But not all of these have been classified as "border industrial areas," the definition of such areas apparently requiring the need for special inducements to attract industry, as is the case for East London, whose economy has been somewhat stagnant. It would, however, be quite easy to alter the definition of border areas to include a much larger part of the existing industrial complex of South Africa, and the temptation to do so in order to demonstrate progress may prove irresistible. Indeed there has already been a fudging of the position in that the Datsun-Nissan auto assembly plant near Pretoria has apparently

[59] These include loans, capital participation, erection of factory buildings, tax rebates, provision of rail facilities, road and rail rate concessions, and wage concessions.

[60] Some observers have seen the border industrial areas as potential Hong Kongs, possibly exacerbating the racial and political scene.

been classified as a border industry although Pretoria is not classed as a border area.[61]

The possibility of including many existing urban centers in the list of border areas exposes the flimsiness of the whole concept. It might, however, conceivably contain the key to later developments, for it would be only one slight step beyond the border concept to declare the large townships such as Soweto (1965 population, 496,000) reserves, or to enlarge a number of reserves to bring their borders closer to the cities.

In summary, it seems reasonably clear that the border industry program will not decrease the existing economic integration of Africans and whites in South Africa, and hence is no alternative to present integration. Furthermore, it does not appear likely that it will materially decrease the flow of Africans to the cities, particularly since the achievements to date have largely been tributary to existing urban areas. And finally, very few industrialists seem to have any interest in furthering the program or in moving their plants from the present centers to border areas.

SUMMARY AND CONCLUSIONS

This paper started with the assumption that support for multilateral sanctions or for military action against South Africa is not sufficiently strong to suggest that these courses are likely to be adopted in the foreseeable future, although it was noted that unpredictable events might reverse this assessment. In the search for alternative ways to further a change in South Africa various measures of disengagement have been propounded by several individuals and organizations. Particular attention has been focused upon economic disengagement, which is often seen as more appropriate than the breaking of cultural and political contacts, which would need to be retained if any kind of dialogue is to be carried on.

An examination of economic disengagement, however, raises cer-

[61] There is also a possibility that the government might decide to force certain industries to move to border areas from their present sites. Officials are reported to have warned in 1965 that, if the trend toward increasing use of Africans in the garment industry in the Transvaal were not reversed, the whole industry might be required to move to border areas.

tain questions, some comparable to those which led to the rejection of sanctions, others applying specifically to disengagement alone or to unilateral disengagement. These include the following: Would economic disengagement be accepted by Africans and other critics of United States policy as an adequate posture, and thus would it improve the credibility of our stance much beyond the stage of imposition? Would it be effective in changing South African policies? Would economic disengagement most hurt those it was intended to aid? Would the African be in a better position in an eventual multiracial state with a greater acquisition of skills and a well-developed economy or under one that has been stunted over a long period of years? Is there a greater chance to alter and expose the faults of apartheid under an open and improving economy or under a program of isolation and disengagement which might induce the government to adopt more rigid group areas, influx control, and job reservation practices?

In attempting to provide partial answers to some of these questions, the extent of U.S. involvement was examined. South African–American economic relations were found to be of relatively minor significance to the United States and not sufficiently important to South Africa for unilateral economic disengagement to have a severe impact on its economy. South African dependence on the United States is most significant in trade and in the quantitative and qualitative contribution of American concerns to its manufacturing sector. In view of the relatively favorable record of manufacturing industries in South Africa with respect to wages and new job opportunities for non-whites, the present and growing emphasis of American investment on manufacturing is not entirely to be deprecated.

In examining the impact of demographic factors and economic growth on South Africa the evidence suggested that both contain forces which are working more or less powerfully against the stated goals of apartheid. Employment of Africans has increased in relation to the white population and considerably more rapidly than the growth of the African population itself. Wages have also shown relative improvement in recent years, particularly in manufacturing and construction. Influx control has not worked effectively, and job reservation rules are being increasingly breached, while the reserve development and border industry programs of apartheid are not offsetting these forces in any significant way. The results are increasing interdependence of the racial groups in South Africa, and increasing detribalization, urbanization, Westernization, and economic integration of the African, despite mounting legal restrictions. Economic growth has made nonsense of apartheid in its most rigid forms.[62] No objective observer would be satisfied with the progress that has been achieved, particularly when so many African families are still living below the poverty datum line. But the assumption that economic forces are the villain in the piece is subject to serious question.

The real difficulty is that increasing economic integration has not led to social and political freedoms for the non-white. There is increased segregation everywhere except on the job, where white and non-white work together in a growing but often unrecognized partnership. Several important questions are posed by these conflicting trends: Will political change be more expedited if economic growth is sustained or if it is retarded? Will the non-white be in a better position to effect change if his material condition is improving or if it is deteriorating?

These questions, which go beyond the scope of this paper, arouse strongly contradictory responses. Quigg, for example, seems to imply that a retarded economy would bring change when he writes that the advance made by some Africans "has much to do with the atmosphere of tranquility that prevails in South Africa today. But let the African's economic frustrations equal his political frustrations, and the Europeans will be in for a shock." [63] Vernon McKay, on the other hand, told the O'Hara Committee that the "record of history shows that the more people advance the more they become conscious of their capacity for further advancement and the more frustrated they are by the arbitrary restrictions that remain." [64] Quigg, too, sees some encouragement in the economic boom in that

[62] Quintin Whyte, director of the South African Institute of Race Relations, wrote in 1965 that "it is becoming obvious that what one might call 'big apartheid" is not succeeding" (*A Survey . . . 1965*, p. 3.)

[63] Quigg, *South Africa*, p. 11.

[64] *United States–South African Relations*, Part I, p. 88.

"it could provide the means to find a resolution of the race problem if there were any disposition to do so on a rational basis." [65]

A final question remains: If economic disengagement were rejected as an appropriate policy for the United States, what alternatives exist? The findings of this paper have been that two rather powerful forces—demographic and economic—are working against apartheid and that economic disengagement would weaken to some degree the second of these forces.[66] It does not follow that the United States should not continue to make it clear that it does not support or accept apartheid. This it must do if it is to remain true to its ideals. Its policy might then be described as one of moral dissociation or selective disengagement. Such a policy could be furthered in a number of ways, including:

1. high-level reiteration that apartheid is not acceptable and that it can only bring trouble to South Africa;
2. efforts to persuade the South African government that apartheid cannot serve our common interests of saving Africa from cold-war conflict, maintaining stability in Africa, and assisting in the development of the newly independent states;
3. assisting in opening a dialogue between South Africa and other African states, possibly by encouraging an exchange program to reduce the mutual ignorance of both sides;
4. adoption by U.S. firms operating in South Africa of policies and practices which reflect an enlightened attitude toward racial conditions, and which recognize their position as representatives of a country which supports human rights and racial equality;
5. fostering objective studies devoted to such subjects as:
   a. the scientific examination of racial attitudes and frictions
   b. the origins, impact, and anatomy of apartheid

[65] Quigg, South Africa, p. 15.
[66] If it is accepted that economic forces are to some degree eroding certain aspects of apartheid it does not necessarily follow that the United States should positively encourage investment in South Africa. The decision whether to invest or not properly rests with the individual concern; the government should doubtless provide information regarding any conditions in South Africa which would have a bearing on the investor, but the present official policy of neither encouraging nor discouraging investment would appear to be the most logical one to follow.

    c. the internal contradictions of apartheid

    d. the falseness of the economic theories employed to support apartheid, and the cost of trying to restrain favorable economic forces

    e. cost of living, household budgets, and wages

    f. achievements or lack thereof of the reserve development and border industry programs;

6. stressing the need for South Africa, if it seeks the understanding of the world, to demonstrate that greater progress is being made by non-whites, and to show that the gaps between all groups are narrowing.

Karis has suggested that "the current United States policy is a mixture that probably satisfies no one." [67] But this conclusion would doubtless fit any policy. The suggestions listed above might at least have the advantage of focusing upon constructive possibilities rather than upon the destructive weapons of war, sanctions, and economic disengagement.

The element of time is of crucial significance in the selection of a United States policy toward South Africa. If a crisis were expected in the Republic in the near future a policy of full dissociation and disengagement would appear to be more practicable and desirable. Indeed there might well be reason to renew the interest in multilateral sanctions worked out carefully in advance of their imposition and with an insistence on universal application.

If the evidence suggests, however, that no crisis is likely to occur in the foreseeable future, then the United States might, by a policy of unilateral economic disengagement, not only reduce its own ability to influence change in South Africa but weaken to some extent those economic forces which are working against certain of the stated goals of apartheid.

[67] Karis, *South Africa*, p. 58.

Editor's Postscript

⟨✵⟩

INVOLVED as it is or may be with the three great confrontations facing the world—that between rich and poor, that between East and West, and that between the races—southern Africa presents a difficult dilemma in the formation of United States policy.

Most Americans who have studied the area find abhorrent the political, economic, and social restriction, segregation, and suppression of the majority black African populations in Portuguese Angola and Mozambique, Rhodesia, and South Africa. While it is hard to believe that the white Rhodesians can maintain dominance over the remaining 95 or 96 percent of that country's population for very long, especially if the world community persists in applying the mandatory sanctions adopted by the United Nations in 1966, and Portugal seems too weak to retain indefinite control over its two large "overseas provinces" in southern Africa, the Republic of South Africa appears to be a white redoubt of increasing strength and one which shows few if any signs of slackening the dominance of its governing minority. South Africa, and particularly the massive framework of repressive laws and customs which comprise its system of apartheid, appears to be the core of the problem as far as the formulation of American policy is concerned.

This is not to say that the weaker white states to the north can be forgotten. McKay points to the facts that they, too, "have developed sufficient military power and determination to maintain varying forms of white supremacy," and that, despite policies which were philosophically widely different, all three ruling groups have tended to coalesce in their stands against black nationalism and in support of continued domination of the whites.

But it is South Africa which has by far the greatest economic and political power, strengthened immeasurably by its much higher ratio of whites to non-whites. And it is South Africa which has built up the most formidable system of suppressive laws and regulations which enshrine segregation as a national policy. As Kuper points out, the concentration of power in the hands of whites and the retention of political initiative by whites have long dominated the political history of South Africa; the present monopoly of political power by whites under apartheid is the logical culmination of this history.

The abhorrence of apartheid, the fear that it may lead to a polarization of African or world conflict along racial lines, the realization that the open sore of racial conditions in South Africa might readily infect relations between the United States and independent African countries, that it might weaken the United Nations, and that it presents a constant invitation for intrusion by Moscow or Peking or at least for attraction to them by nationalist movements in southern Africa—all these factors create a strong wish to find some reasonable policy which would have and could be seen to have an effect on changing the dangerous trends in South Africa.

But adequate spontaneous change seems highly unlikely and the ability to change the situation by outside persuasion or intervention appears, on examination, to be pitifully inadequate to the task. Indeed, all the potential forces for possibly rapid change appear to have weakened in recent years. Internally, as McKay sees it, "suppression of Africans is eroding away the leadership of the middle class," and some Africans have concluded that they must learn to tolerate the situation. Kuper notes that, historically, non-white political action has been essentially defensive, which he explains as a reaction to white initiatives, as a result of the armed strength of the whites and the disarming of the non-whites, and as a reflection of the lack of unity among the non-whites. This lack of unity is now intensified by apartheid, which "inevitably channels much activity toward separatism." And Kuper concludes: "At present, there is little evidence of political opposition by Africans inside the country."

Meanwhile, the white oligarchy displays increasing solidity and strength. The unification of this oligarchy is one of Munger's main themes; he opines that "there exists in the country an even greater polarization of white and black than at any previous period" and that the "government has been strengthened in its views that might must be white."

Externally, the forces which might bring sufficient weight are weak and divided. As McKay points out, there is growing frustration among the exiles, the independent states north of the Zambezi lack the military and logistic capability of intervening, the United Nations is not a promising organ for military or even economic measures, and neither the United Kingdom nor the United States wishes to use military force or to assume the burden of effecting a change.

Some changes affecting the balance of power are observable, including the increasingly dispassionate and rational way in which Africans outside the Republic now expand and refine methods for a long-term campaign, the growing economic strength of the Africans within South Africa, the professed desire of the South African government to build bridges to the rest of Africa which, to be successful, would require some evidence of evolution toward a more reasonable racial policy, and, in the long run, the changing demographic ratios in the country.

A variety of factors have tended to reduce the pressure on South Africa in recent years. In addition to those already noted these include the involvement of both East and West in other parts of the world, a decline in their competition in tropical Africa, the inconclusive decision of the World Court in the South West African case, the desire to prevent all of the problems of southern Africa reaching a simultaneous crescendo, a growing wish to reduce American involvement in various parts of the world, and at least some support for Rhodesia and South Africa from conservatives in the United States, witnessed by the intense mobilization of conservative propaganda in this country. The prospect for encouraging change is also doubtlessly reduced by the inability to suggest a policy that would allay the fears of the whites in South Africa, which helps to explain the tenacity with which that country's government, in

McKay's words, "clings steadfastly to rigid enforcement of racial segregation as its basic policy."

In searching for changes within South Africa which might conceivably lead to some more acceptable adjustment among the races (and most people would agree with McKay that no solution to the South African problem is likely unless a policy based on consent is devised), none of the authors find great hope.

Munger does discern among the whites a growing "political, human, and economic consciousness of the African's position in society" and notes "that white and black groups are now facing each other without intermediate translators." He also concludes that the period when white men speak for Africans has ended; sees increased participation in some of the churches, in running the African townships, and even in company operations; and cites an example of the Transkei Parliament acting contrary to the wishes of the Nationalist government.

Munger also detects certain new voices rising among South African whites and tentative moves toward the formulation of a new foreign policy, resulting in part from the successful achievement of the main Afrikaner goals, the unification of the white oligarchy, and some success in conducting relations with the former High Commission Territories and Malawi. Possible results of these changing perspectives include a wider recognition that South Africa is a part of Africa and must act accordingly, an increased understanding of the desires and value systems of other people in Africa, the creation of a bridge to the Coloured population, and movement toward the creation of a "larger laager."

But Munger is cautious in predicting notable changes resulting from the complex of trends within the white South African community. The "emergence of a new kind of black voice . . . does not necessarily mean significant internal change is on the horizon"; the new white voices "may dissipate or be quenched"; the foreign policy is "still too new to be judged success or failure"; "the fact that there is change . . . is no guarantee it will be for the better or for the worse." He also notes that the South African plea to be given time has long been made "without resulting in major steps toward solving the problem." McKay also opines that "the much publicized 'flexibility' and 'pragmatism' of Prime Minister B. J. Vorster have not in any way even approached . . . [the] fundamental problem" of giving non-whites political rights in the white areas commensurate with their economic status.

Kuper notes the somewhat remarkable fact that, despite the increasing separatism in South Africa, the "overriding influence in African political thought has been the emphasis on interracialism," explained mainly "by a gravitational pull . . . toward the interracial core of society," and which is "most consistent with the economic and social structure of South African society." Most consistent because the processes of change have brought "increasing contact and interdependence," "encouraged social interaction between members of different groups," and "fostered a mutual acculturation."

But he concludes that apartheid seeks to reverse "these processes of social interweaving and cultural communication" and that "under conditions of a virtual monopoly of political power by whites . . . the ideologies of non-whites are likely to be of minor significance within South Africa."

The editor, too, sees certain potentially favorable changes in the position of the African, primarily through increased participation in the booming South African economy and witnessed in a higher ratio of wage employment, improving wages, and promotion to more skilled jobs by abrogation of job reservation edicts. But while the African is increasingly urbanized, industrialized, and economically integrated, and while such economic aspects of apartheid as influx control, job reservation, the border industry program, and the reserve development plans are seen as subject to very great economic and demographic pressure, the facts remain that there is "increased segregation everywhere except on the job," written and unwritten impediments to African advance have proliferated, and political concessions are limited to the extension of partial self-government under the controversial Bantustan program.

There is some difference of opinion among the authors with respect to the strength of economic forces and the likelihood of their effecting a change in South Africa. McKay believes that the "effects of industrialization on a rigid pattern are only marginal and indirect" and that economic integration will not "kill apartheid." Kuper does not see the process of industrialization altering the social structure and notes that the competition at the less-skilled level resulting from industrialization may even contribute to the increasingly repressive policies of the political system. The editor, too, holds no great hopes for economic forces being strong enough to bring significant political change, though he does not see economic growth contributing to the strength of apartheid and delineates a variety of ways in which economic forces are altering or conflicting with the *economic* aspects of apartheid.

Several of the authors see economic forces as being of possibly greater significance in the long run. McKay opines that to the extent that industrialization "results in economic advancement it makes Africans more conscious of their capacity to advance." Kuper concludes that a major source of change within South African society "is likely to be in the tension between the economic and political systems," with the elite strata among subordinate groups renewing pressure for political change and "some responsiveness among certain strata of whites." The editor feels that demographic factors and economic growth "contain forces which are working more or less powerfully against the stated goals of apartheid."

Changes are, then, taking place both within and outside South Africa, but they provide separately or in combination little hope for a rapid improvement in the position of the South African blacks.

In the meantime there has been a narrowing of the options for American policy, at least a narrowing of those which are both acceptable and reasonably likely of adoption. The dilemma is, therefore, a painful and frustrating one, because none of the options or measures are likely to have a really significant impact on the problem.

All of the authors are agreed that pressure and persuasion should not be relaxed. Some progress may be made by appealing to the white South Africans' pride of achievement, professed religious principles, sense of fair play, such liberalism as exists, and their desire for continuing economic advance. There are also aspects of the South African economic and social scene which should be improved and which have no inherent connection with the so-called philosophy of apartheid, such as wage levels below the poverty datum line and certain educational and social facilities. Attention can also profitably continue to be given to the uneconomic aspects of apartheid and other internal inconsistencies whose elimination would benefit all people in South Africa.

Finally, the four authors agree that the United States must continue to stand by its long and deeply held principles and ideals supporting human rights and racial equality. The time factor may have stretched out in South Africa by recent internal and external events and changes, but time is not permanently on the side of racial restrictions and suppression.

Selected Bibliography

◄✵►

Austin, Dennis. *Britain and South Africa.* London, Oxford University Press for the Royal Institute of International Affairs, 1966.

British Council of Churches. *The Future of South Africa: A Study by British Christians.* Ed. by T. A. Beetham and N. Salter. London, SCM Press, 1965.

Brown, Douglas. *Against the World: A Study of White South African Attitudes.* London, Collins, 1966.

Bunting, Brian P. *The Rise of the South African Reich.* Harmondsworth, Middlesex, Penguin Books, 1964.

Calvocoressi, Peter. *South Africa and World Opinion.* London, Oxford University Press for the Institute of Race Relations, 1961.

Carstens, W. P. *The Social Structure of a Cape Coloured Reserve: A Study of Racial Integration and Segregation in South Africa.* London, Oxford University Press, 1966.

D'Amato, Anthony A. "The Bantustan Proposals for South-West Africa," *Journal of Modern African Studies,* IV, No. 2 (1967), 177–92.

Davis, John A., and James K. Baker. *Southern Africa in Transition.* New York, Frederick A. Praeger for the American Society of African Culture, 1966.

De Kiewiet, C. W. *The Anatomy of South African Misery.* London, Oxford University Press, 1956.

deVilliers, H. H. W. *Rivonia: Operation Mayibuye.* Johannesburg, Afrikaanse Pers-boekhandel, 1964.

Doxey, G. V. *The Industrial Colour Bar in South Africa.* London, Oxford University Press, 1961.

Duffy, James. *Portuguese Africa.* Cambridge, Mass., Harvard University Press, 1962.

Emerson, Rupert. *Africa and United States Policy.* Englewood Cliffs, N.J., Prentice-Hall, 1967.

First, Ruth. *South West Africa.* Baltimore, Penguin Books, 1963.

Gross, Ernest A. "The South West Africa Case: What Happened," *Foreign Affairs*, XLV, No. 1 (October, 1966), 36–48.

Higgins, Rosalyn. *The Development of International Law through the Political Organs of the United Nations*. London, Oxford University Press for the Royal Institute of International Affairs, 1963.

Horrell, Muriel, comp. *Survey of Race Relations in South Africa* (annual). Johannesburg, South African Institute of Race Relations.

Hoskins, Lewis M. "South Africa's Diplomatic Offensive: Change and Continuity," *East Africa Journal*, August, 1967, pp. 17–22.

Houghton, D. Hobart. *The South African Economy*. Cape Town, Oxford University Press, 1964.

Hutt, William H. *The Economics of the Colour Bar*. London, Andre Deutsch, for Institute of Economic Affairs, 1964.

Karis, Thomas. *South Africa: The End Is Not Yet*. New York, Foreign Policy Association, Headline Series No. 176, 1966.

Krause, Otto. "Vorster and the Future of Nationalist Policy," *Optima*, December, 1966, pp. 171–77.

Kuper, Hilda. *Indian People in Natal*. Durban, Natal University Press, 1960.

Kuper, Leo. *An African Bourgeoisie: Race, Class and Politics in South Africa*. New Haven, Yale University Press, 1965.

Legum, Colin, and Margaret Legum. *South Africa: Crisis for the West*. New York, Frederick A. Praeger, 1964.

Leiss, Amelia C., ed. *Apartheid and United Nations Collective Measures*. New York, Carnegie Endowment for International Peace, 1965.

Lewin, Julius. *Politics and Law in South Africa: Essays on Race Relations*. New York, Monthly Review Press, 1963.

Marquard, Leo. *The Peoples and Policies of South Africa*. 3d ed. London, Oxford University Press, 1962.

Mezerik, A. G., ed. *Rhodesia and the United Nations*. New York, International Review Service, 1966.

Munger, Edwin S. *Afrikaner and African Nationalism: South African Parallels and Parameters*. London, New York, Cape Town, Oxford University Press, 1967.

—— *Bechuanaland: Pan African Outpost or Bantu Homeland*. London, Oxford University Press, 1965.

—— *Notes on the Formation of South African Foreign Policy*. Pasadena, Castle Press, 1965.

Ngubane, Jordan K. *An African Explains Apartheid*. New York, Frederick A. Praeger, 1963.

Nielsen, Waldemar. *African Battleline: American Policy Choices in Southern Africa*. New York, Harper, for the Council on Foreign Relations, 1965.

Quigg, Philip W. *South Africa: Problems and Prospects.* New York, The Council on Religion and International Affairs, 1965.

Republic of South Africa. *South West Africa Survey, 1967.* Pretoria, Government Printer, 1967.

—— Commission of Enquiry into South West Africa Affairs. *Report, 1962–1963.* Pretoria, Government Printer, 1964.

Sacks, Benjamin. *South Africa: An Imperial Dilemma (Non-Europeans and the British Nation, 1902–1914).* Albuquerque, University of New Mexico Press, 1967.

Segal, Ronald, ed. *Economic Sanctions against South Africa.* London, Penguin Books, 1964.

Spence, J. E. *Republic under Pressure: A Study of South African Foreign Policy.* London, Oxford University Press for the Royal Institute of International Affairs, 1965.

Spooner, F. P. *South African Predicament: The Economics of Apartheid.* New York, Frederick A. Praeger, 1962.

Thompson, Leonard. *The Republic of South Africa.* Boston, Little, Brown, and Co., 1966.

UNESCO. *The Effects of "Apartheid" on Education, Science, Culture and Information in South Africa.* Draft, January 18, 1967. In press.

United Nations General Assembly. *Reports of the Special Committee on the Policies of Apartheid of the Government of the Republic of South Africa.* UN Documents A/5497; A/6486; A/Ac-115/L.56 Rev. 2.

United States–South African Relations. Hearings before the Subcommittee on Africa of the Committee on Foreign Affairs, House of Representatives, Parts I–IV. Washington: Government Printing Office, 1966.

Van Den Berghe, Pierre L. *South Africa: A Study in Conflict.* Middletown, Conn., Wesleyan University Press, 1965.

Vulindela, Mtshali, B. *Rhodesia: Background to Conflict.* New York, Hawthorn Books, 1967.

Young, Kenneth. *Rhodesia and Independence.* London, Eyre and Spottiswoode, 1967.